Musings, Meanderings, and Monsters, Too

Essays on Academic Librarianship

edited by
Martin H. Raish

The Scarecrow Press, Inc.
Lanham, Maryland, and Oxford
2003

SCARECROW PRESS, INC.

Published in the United States of America
by Scarecrow Press, Inc.
A Member of the Rowman & Littlefield Publishing Group
4501 Forbes Boulevard, Suite 200, Lanham, MD 20706
www.scarecrowpress.com

PO Box 317
Oxford
OX2 9RU, UK

British Library Cataloguing in Publication Information Available

Library of Congress Cataloging-in-Publication Data

Raish, Martin.
  Musings, meanderings, and monsters, too : essays on academic
librarianship / [edited by] Martin H. Raish.
    p. cm.
  Includes bibliographical references.
  ISBN 0-8108-4767-1 (alk. paper)
 1. Academic libraries—Aims and objectives. 2. Academic
libraries—Automation. 3. Libraries—Special collections—Electronic
information resources. 4. Information literacy—Study and teaching
(Higher). 5. Libraries and education. I. Title.
Z675.U5R175 2003
027.7—dc21
                                    2003002085

♾ ™ The paper used in this publication meets the minimum requirements of
American National Standard for Information Sciences—Permanence of
Paper for Printed Library Materials, ANSI/NISO Z39.48-1992.
Manufactured in the United States of America.

Contents

Acknowledgments

This volume would never have come into being without the efforts of my sixteen colleagues who wrote the essays. They transformed an idea into a reality, and were wonderful companions who made the journey as stimulating and enlightening as the final product.

Sue Eason of Scarecrow Press provided the gentle persuasion and encouragement I needed to complete the task.

Don Norton and his students in the Brigham Young University Faculty Editing Services exercised their outstanding editorial skills to hone and polish the essays.

Thank you to all.

Introduction: Monsters in Our Closets

It does not do to leave a live dragon out of your calculations, if you live near him.

—J. R. R. Tolkien, *The Hobbit*

Do you remember as a child lying awake at night wondering what sort of creatures lurked just a few feet away, ready to leap out of your closet and torture you without mercy? Do you want to give a librarian the same kind of cold sweats? Just bring up the subject of e-books or e-journals (or e-anything), or mention the word "virtual," as in the "virtual library," or the phrase "information technology." Even in the bright light of day these words will raise anxiety and blood pressure, if not cause outright panic.

And they are the sort of monsters this collection of essays is about.

The project did not begin with monsters in mind. When I invited colleagues to contribute to this collection, the only topic I mentioned was "the modern academic library." My vision was of a book that would be wide-ranging, intriguing, and thought provoking—that would pique our colleagues' curiosity and perhaps help them see academic library issues in a new light. I was looking for essays that were more than opinion pieces but less than research papers. As the essays began to come in, I was delighted to see that they had precisely these qualities. But I also saw the monsters.

Two beasts that rear their fiendish heads most often among the essays are technology and change. The spiraling need to teach students critical-thinking skills is another frightening prospect, especially as we see the need to do more but are faced with ever limited resources. Educating librarians for the tasks ahead is equally worrisome.

Some of the concerns addressed in these essays are like aggressive ogres, while others are more like friendly giants. But all are dragons that we live near; we cannot leave them out of our calculations. We could try pretending they don't really exist. We could keep our eyes focused straight ahead and continue doing the things we've always done, in the same ways we've always done them—following the same formulas and policies and hoping the monsters will leave us alone.

Or we could hire someone else to take care of them for us. We could outsource our defense to mercenary soldiers, but we fear losing control by letting outsiders into our library to look in the closets even more than we fear the monsters themselves.

No, we must face the dragons ourselves. These essays offer excellent advice on how we might accomplish this. Some focus on libraries and librarians by looking at how our profession has been altered by external forces and suggesting ways to cope with these forces. Others center their attention on students by recommending how we can help them learn to live effectively in the Age of Information.

Some of the counsel is pragmatic; some is philosophical. Most of the writers approach their particular monster from the direction of the reference desk or the library-instruction program (mostly because I solicited essays primarily from colleagues I knew via the bibliographic-instruction listserv, or BI-L), but even these show a diversity of attitudes and solutions. All the essays are written by experienced academic librarians who have collectively devoted more than a few centuries to learning how to cope with "the information explosion," its resultant computerization of resources, and its recently developed transportation medium—the World Wide Web.

You will probably find some ideas here that you wholeheartedly agree with and some that are a bit disquieting. All of the essays will make you think, and my hope is that, in spite of the advice of Bilbo Baggins that one should "never laugh at live dragons," you will also find some that bring you a smile.

A note about the quotations. Those that appear at the beginning of each essay were provided by the individual authors to set the stage for their musings. Those that appear after the essays were selected by me, not necessarily because they enhance the authors' ideas, but simply because I like them. Some are delicate desserts to complement a sumptuous main course, while others are more like impish monsters that poke you in your stomach (or brain). All are from my files gathered over the past thirty-five years in academe. I hope you enjoy them as much as I have.

One ought, every day at least, to hear a little song, read a good poem, see a fine picture, and, if it were possible, to speak a few reasonable words.

—Goethe

CHAPTER ONE

Academic Librarians Offer the Crucial Human Element in Online Scholarship[1]

Martin Raish

> Technology makes things possible. People make things happen.
>
> —Erich Block

In the 1957 film *Desk Set*, a group of librarians (led by Katharine Hepburn) squares off against an efficiency expert (Spencer Tracy) who has been hired to install a large computer in their corporate library. They are fearful that their skills as researchers and information experts will be devalued—that they may even be replaced by the "electronic brain." That is not the plan, Tracy assures them. The Electromagnetic Memory and Research Arithmetical Calculator (EMMARAC), affectionately called Miss Emmy, "is not going to take over," he says. "It's just here to help you."

Those words proved true for Hepburn and her staff, but will they for academic librarians today? The Internet and the World Wide Web (the

Web) are transforming physical libraries into virtual ones, which play new roles and require librarians to perform tasks they had not dreamed of when they were in library school. Most disquieting is that some of the new activities threaten to undermine values that librarians have honored and defended since the days of Melvil Dewey. The result is anxiety, and even fear.

It is not so much that we might lose our jobs—the justifiable concern of the *Desk Set* librarians—but that technology is requiring us to assume new roles and duties, while not allowing us to surrender any of the old ones. We still must answer questions from patrons who come to our buildings, but we must also deal with those who send us e-mail requests. We barely learn the idiosyncrasies of one new database before we have to master two more—and have to teach students and colleagues how to use all three. As such demands increase, how will we maintain our high standards of service?

Traditionally, librarians have focused on four core activities: identifying, acquiring, making available, and preserving the records of civilization. Looking at the ways technology has affected those activities reveals how well machines such as EMMARAC have been able to, as Tracy promised Hepburn and her colleagues, "liberate [our] time for more important work."

It has always been a challenge to identify materials to acquire. Even the richest libraries have struggled to buy both new books and older materials they had missed in the past. When libraries' collections were mostly paper, librarians could rely on well-established guidelines and trusted tools to help in the identification and selection process—compilations of books in print, bibliographies, book reviews, and so forth. Those sources remain useful for printed material, but they are not sufficient for—nor even particularly relevant to—online resources. With the publicly available material on the Web approaching a billion pages, not even Superman (or Yahoo, Google, or any other Web search engine or database) knows what is out there. Nor does anybody know what would be appropriate for a library to collect. As a well-known New Yorker cartoon by Peter Steiner puts it, "On the Internet, nobody knows you're a dog."

Even after we have identified some online material that we want, what does it mean to acquire it in cyberspace? Web databases are assemblages of disembodied pixels not tangible things that can be placed on a shelf.

Remember the green volumes of the *Readers Guide to Periodical Literature* in your college library? For nearly a century, librarians bought those, and dozens of more narrowly focused indexes to journal literature, directly from the index publishers. Today, we deal with aggregators, companies that compile online databases containing dozens of such indexes. Many index publishers sell their products to several aggregators, yet no two aggregators offer the same sets of indexes in their databases—so a library may be forced to pay for access to a particular index three or four times, to get access to all of those needed. If a library decides to change aggregators, it may eliminate some duplication, but it may also lose access to some material. As a result, the collection changes constantly, in both content and mode of access, creating confusion for patrons and librarians.

Acquiring online journals can be an even bigger headache. In a paper-based world, it did not matter if the publisher moved to a new headquarters—mail traveled from the publisher to the library, whose street address had not changed. But now the flow is in the opposite direction for the thousands of electronic journals that already exist: We librarians must contact publishers to maintain our collections, and if their websites move, how are we to know? Sometimes we find out only when a student shows us that a particular site no longer works.

EMMARAC and her progeny have undeniably made it easier and quicker for librarians to make material available to patrons. Electronic access is especially valuable to off-site users, who can look through databases, download material, view images, read full texts of articles, and use other resources that a decade ago were all but inaccessible to them—or at least available only after a considerable delay. Some technical details have proved difficult to master, and we have had to rely heavily on non-librarians to make electronic delivery work, but for the most part, librarians now have an easier time of getting material to users.

The last traditional activity of librarians, that of preserving material for future generations, illustrates most clearly the sea change facing libraries in the twenty-first century. Again, the situation with electronic journals indicates the scope of the problem. The key question is, who owns the back files of journals?

In the past, the norm was that subscribers to print journals owned the copies they had purchased, and retained all of those copies, even if the library canceled its subscription or the publisher stopped producing the journal. But what happens in the electronic world, where back issues are on the publisher's computer rather than physically within the walls of the library? Will the publisher assume the role of an archive, preserving the digital files indefinitely—even if the files have little commercial value and occupy valuable computer space? Or will that task fall to librarians? Will we have access to all back issues, or only to those we once owned? And who will make sure that the material remains accessible, when software, hardware, storage media, and telecommunications systems change?

While some publishers are becoming archives, some libraries are turning into publishers. Academic libraries are finding themselves under increasing pressure from campus administrators and professors to accept publishing as a significant part of their mission. Many treasures have lain hidden for years in special collections, accessible only to limited audiences and under restricted rules of use. But digital cameras and the Web have made it possible to create virtual collections of manuscripts, journals, photographs, artworks, and almost anything else.

For administrators, digitization solves the problem of how to make such materials more available to a wider audience—especially distance-education students and researchers in remote locations—while at the same time protecting them from deterioration through being handled too often.

Professors want librarians to digitize such material as dissection models for biology classes, architectural diagrams for art-history students, and collections of artifacts from archaeological digs. Faculty members are also asking librarians to place the full texts of an increasing number of articles on electronic reserve, requiring the librarians to spend much more time negotiating with publishers and authors about copyright clearances and permission fees.

Digitizing images and texts requires skills in computer programming not normally taught in library school, as well as an understanding of the confusing—and shifting—terrain of copyright law for electronic materials. Here, again, we are working more and more with nonlibrarians, a situation that can lead to differences in priorities and misunderstandings of how things should be done. Should we fill a vacancy in the cataloging department, or create a new position for a Web manager, or a supervisor of copyrights and fair use? Should we buy more public catalog terminals, or upgrade the workstations in our offices?

Together, those changes are having a profound impact on academic librarianship. EMMARAC and her descendants not only have caused tremendous revisions in the day-to-day practices of the profession but also have forced significant paradigm shifts.

The "just-in-case" collections of the past—those that tried to anticipate users' needs by building the largest and deepest collections possible—have given way to the "just-in-time" model of today: We may not have what you need right here in the building, but we can get it for you quickly. Maneuvering from the first paradigm to the second has not been easy or comfortable, and now a third is emerging. It is the "just-for-me" library, where I, as the patron, can customize almost everything to fit my personal needs and quirks.

In the "just-for-me" library, the catalog will not bother me with links to databases I don't use: It will eliminate them on my personalized interface. On the other hand, the system will notify me of new books in my areas of interest, suggest related works, and offer other features from an extensive menu—just as online booksellers already do. While those dot-coms are not directly driving the paradigm shift, they have created expectations among students that existing library catalogs cannot meet. Creating the successor to the current online catalog—the "one-stop-shopping" library-information portal—is one of two essential tasks for academic librarians in the next ten years.

The last time we faced a similar situation, we failed to respond. The first Web search engines were developed by nonlibrarians, and, because of that, we have spent a great deal of time and energy trying to make searching the Web work the way we believe it should have worked from the beginning. We know the value of carefully constructed searches using terms gleaned from specialized lists, and we are horrified when students enter a word or two in a box, hit the enter key, and are happy with the 35,174 items they retrieve. We value accuracy and completeness; our students value speed and convenience.

Regardless of how strongly we want to cling to our better ways of finding information, if we fail a second time to create the sort of library tools that today's students want, someone else will produce them. The result will be that the library will increasingly become the source of last resort, rather than the first.

The second essential task for librarians over the next few years is to help our students become information literate.

A familiar adage tells us, "If you give a man a fish, you feed him for a day, but if you teach him how to fish, you feed him for a lifetime." What we are doing with all our technological infrastructure is akin to giving a fisherman a huge, powerful, new boat, with lots of fancy new nets and rods and sonar and other equipment. Sometimes, we also give the fisherman access to improved technological training—we show him how to start the engine, steer, lower and raise the nets, and so forth.

Too often, though, we do not help him answer such questions as, Where do I go to find the best fishing? What places should I avoid because of dangers or lack of fish? What are the best ways to fish—trawling or standing still, casting my nets near the surface or deeper down? How do I know which of the fish that I catch are good, and how can I separate them from the bad? How do I preserve the fish I need for later use? If my circumstances change, how can I take what I know about fishing and apply it to farming? How can I teach my skills to my children or my neighbors?

We need to do more than simply teach students how to do high-quality research for their classes. We must prepare them to thrive in to-day's information-rich environment, to succeed as individuals, parents, workers, and citizens.

I have painted a rather cheerless picture of academic librarianship, but I have not been entirely fair. Along with the challenges of change have come significant benefits. For example, using computer databases has many advantages over searching paper indexes. Several users can search the same resources at the same time and look through multiple years (or even multiple indexes) in a single search. As searching software becomes better at extracting meaning, rather than just words, from texts, the probability of finding relevant material is improving.

Similarly, the enormous growth of distance-education programs has created the need for us to make our resources available to off-site users. When our efforts have succeeded, we have gained new respect from faculty members and administrators. After having been barely visible on the campus for decades, librarians are now finding themselves sought after for their expertise in finding information and navigating the Web.

The binary world expects librarians to be either for technology or against it. But I hope we will be neither. We must not be neo-Luddites who continue to do the same things in the same ways, regardless of what new things and new ways appear. Nor ought we to be cheerleaders for the techno-utopians who declare that the book is dead and that the library belongs on the endangered-species list. We should reread Sven Birkerts's *The Gutenberg Elegies: The Fate of Reading in an Electronic Age*, but perhaps we should try it as an e-book. We must remember T. S. Eliot's thirst for "the knowledge we have lost in information," but continue to seek it in the wired world. Technology may be the cause of many of the problems we are facing, but it is also their solution.

By the end of *Desk Set*, the librarians arrive at a tentative truce with EMMARAC. The success of their future working relationship is assured when a telephone caller asks a very difficult question. "That's the sort of thing you can spend months finding," Hepburn laments to Tracy. Then she looks at Miss Emmy and back at Tracy. "Might as well give her a crack at it," he suggests.

Because this is a Tracy–Hepburn romance, we all know that the machine will help them fall in love and that they will live happily ever after. I don't know if librarians and computer technology will always enjoy the same wedded bliss, but I'm confident that we can succeed if we put our hearts, minds, processors, and memory chips into it.

Note

1. This is the essay that was the genesis of this collection. It appeared in the April 21, 2000, issue of *The Chronicle of Higher Education* and caught the eye of Sue Easun of Scarecrow Press. She urged me to write "more like it," but I knew that I did not have the time to devote to such an undertaking. I also knew that there were many of my colleagues who could help, so I invited several to join me in this enterprise. You will soon discover that my faith was not misplaced.

In re-reading my words more than two years after they first appeared in print, I am struck by how they outline the issues that the other essayists address in this volume, such as e-resources, collection building, preservation, and information literacy.

My original title for the essay was "Has Technology Changed the Academic Library? Let EMMARAC Count the Ways." *The Chronicle* title gives my words a slightly different twist, but probably a better one, at that.

In its original form, it did not include a leading quotation. I have added one here to match the style of the other essays.

Everybody in the ship menaces us with the prospect of a very "good time" in India. A good time means going to the races, drinking cocktails, dancing till four in the morning, and talking about nothing. And meanwhile the beautiful, the incredible world in which we live awaits our exploration, and life is short, and time flows stanchlessly, like blood from a mortal wound. And there is all knowledge, all art. There are men and women, the innumerable living, and, in books, the souls of those dead who deserved to be immortal. Heaven preserve me, in such a world, from having a Good Time!

—Aldous Huxley, *Jesting Pilate*, 1926

CHAPTER TWO

Slipping Sanctuaries

Amanda Cain

[I]t is essential to begin by reckoning with the fact that one of the foundations of Western culture is leisure. That much, at least, can be learnt from the first chapter of Aristotle's *Metaphysics*. And even the history of the word attests the fact: for leisure in Greek is "skole," and in Latin "scola," the English "school." The word used to designate the place where we educate and teach is derived from a word which means "leisure."

"School" does not, properly speaking, mean school, but leisure.

—Josef Pieper

My university campus resembles less and less a place where a person might go to think. Electric, red Coke machines, MasterCard sign-up stalls, online-workshop flyers, and big-screen sports television throb at every turn. The onslaught of clatter grows worse every semester. I am saved from utter distraction only because my office happens to be behind the heavy doors of the library, one of the university's last sanctuaries for quiet thought.

Providing the academic community with places for quiet thought is a major part of every university's business. Thought is the essence of humanity, and the human prospect is contingent on people having the chance to engage in thought, unhurried. We can safely assume that the world's problems will be more complex and more disheartening tomorrow. If there are no opportunities for careful, hesitant, receptive thought, humankind is damned to a less-than-human existence.[1] "Listening in order to hear" ultimately grants humans the opportunity to improve their lot through creative expression. Shelley describes this hopeful prospect in "To a Skylark":

> Like a poet hidden
> In the light of thought,
> Singing hymns unbidden,
> Till the world is wrought
> To sympathy with hopes and fears it heeded not . . .
> Teach me half the gladness
> That thy brain must know,
> Such harmonious madness
> From my lips would flow,
> The world should listen then, as I am listening now.

Understanding and accepting humanity's worst and grandest in a way that commits our everyday actions to the greater good takes incredible focus and concentration, as well as a free play of wonder and appreciation. These undistracted habits of mind require nothing less than time and space set apart from the workaday world.

Our human ancestors, both mythical and real, sought out the clouds, the ark, the observatories, the banyan tree, the sepulcher, the mountaintop, the *templum*, the room of one's own. They set off to those destinations for revelation and contemplation, to feel greater than the group, and to realize their smallness in the universe. Richard of Saint Victor, an eleventh-century prior, proclaimed the intellectual and moral importance of such quests:

Let a man then rise up to the heart's high place, climb up the mountain if he desire to attain and know what is above the human mind. Let him rise up by himself above himself, and from self-knowledge to the knowledge of God. . . . The ascent of the mountain . . . belongs to self-knowledge; the things done upon the mountain tend to the knowledge of God. Certainly the first are Joseph's, the latter are Benjamin's. . . . A mind which does not raise itself to consideration of its own nature, how can it fly away on the wings of contemplation to that which is above itself? . . . When, do you think, shall a mind which is divided by many desires, and distracted by many thoughts, one way and another, receive this grace? If it has not yet been able to gather itself together into a unity, and does not yet know how to enter into itself, when will it be able to ascend by contemplation to those things which are above itself?[2]

In its history, the university—with its classical, monastic, or natured settings—has also served as a quintessential space for thought. Expressly, it has been an ivory tower where a student might look up and look down, alone, and take his or her bearing on the universe. But this function is slighted more and more in an age that demands material results: the utilitarian, the legislated, the countable, the visible, the noisiest in the bustle and stir. At present, writes Adam Podgorecki, "scholars who take pains with their work, who are full of hesitation, who are troubled by conditional quantifiers and who feel themselves restricted by practical requirements . . . are pushed to the margins."[3] Mankind's future does not beg for hasty and showy improvements, however. If new generations are to arrive at new perspectives and realize better realities, they must face the future with the ability to cultivate long-standing love and deep-rooted wisdom. Developing abilities for untrammeled and full-capacity thinking and imagining is the primary duty of a university; all other university activities should grow out of this enterprise. Higher education's ultimate service to the community depends on this less visible, less noisy role.[4]

Despite this urgent need to do less, campuses are bustling with the "pathos of activity."[5] The notion of the ivory tower has been duly leveled in the name of equity and access, but it has also been brought down in an effort to make the university more visibly occupied with the society at large. Society is experiencing an astonishing increase in and acceleration of technological change, productivity, and commercialism—what Birkerts describes as "so many layers of signals, noises, devices," "habits," and "rates of activity undreamed of by the most animated of philosophers." This massive systemic speed-up is creeping into the environs of some campuses and is being wholly embraced on others. In this new "ethos of busyness," the citizenry's centers for thought are at risk.[6] Faculty members are straining under heavy teaching loads and service requirements; they race to keep up with the explosion of information in their fields; and they are pressed to stay busy producing and marketing their ideas from the perspective of defending, maintaining, and proving their functionality to the society supporting them. They are often too busy for the armchair—too busy to look inward, to meditate, to hesitate, and to thoughtfully develop original accounts of their inquiry.[7]

Students spend less time in school-related activities and sustained recreational reading, and more time financing "the fun industries going full blast."[8] In turn, they spend an increasing amount of time in employment to pay down debt. When college students are in school, their education is subject to frequent changes in legislative initiatives and institutional marketing campaigns. As universities move toward online learning initiatives, for example, private, hesitant thought becomes especially vulnerable. As a reference librarian at one of the country's "most wired" universities, I witness students spending hours troubleshooting our university's new "cutting-edge" "learner-centered" software program just to submit class writing assignments. I watch them bow to bleeps, blinks, and error messages in order to document their learning experiences on the networked server. Their "discussions" in "chat spaces" and online "activity areas" (carried out on reference-area computers) are rushed and raucous with mouse clicks, the movement of fingers, and the glares of screens.[9] Observing all this in a library makes me agree with Stephen Krashen: access to the phenomenally focused combination of "books and comfort and quiet are rarely met in many students' lives, in school or outside of school."[10] In this milieu, we educators give students little chance for, or awareness of, "the quiet stir of thought."

Other forms of technological, administrative, and programmatic busyness include the recent rash of reinventing assessment measures. The unremitting "shifts" and "movements" in this performance industry seem to dominate current administrative vision and supersede the mental composure of students and faculty. Complex, creative, and problem-solving tasks that require concentration, introspection, and careful attention to detail are no doubt adversely affected as academics, in the words of Patricia Broadfoot, "are running hard to stand still" with regard to assessment.[11] It is no wonder that students have difficulty cherishing the highly focused tasks of reading and writing when every sign of their mental activity demands documentation. Nor is it a surprise that faculty increasingly transmit perfunctory work to the academic community (and to the academic library's book shelves and databases).

In the midst of this distracting fuss, university administrators are calling for an increased emphasis on undergraduate involvement in the mentally exacting exercise of research.[12] The stages of the research process have been documented or described by numerous thinkers across the disciplinary spectrum. Christine Hult asserts that the process is generally divided into four stages, regardless of discipline: preparation, incubation, illumination, and verification. Furthermore, the conclusion of the research process comes "only after much conscious study and preparation in conjunction with subconscious intuition."[13] Alas, Hult's consideration of dimensions such as "incubation" or "subconscious intuition" is rare in recent assessment initiatives. Current educational objectives, such as those "performance indicators" listed in the Association of College and Research Libraries' Information Literacy Competency Standards for Higher Education, favor measurable "outcomes."[14] Little if any consideration is given to the silent, internal, and delayed dimensions of scholarship such as wonder and appreciation, incubation and gestation, reflection and illumination—commonplace junctures in the deep and silent reading of printed books. While the rest of the university community is chasing and laying claim to the measurable in scholarship—through inventive portfolios, studies, surveys, and computer-based testing—might not the library continue as it has done for generations and quietly support powerful habits and conditions of scholarship?

"The library protects and encourages a very special kind of life, the life of the mind," writes the distinguished library-science professor, Jesse Shera.[15] Indeed, the quiet and often comfortable environment of a library allows for the concentration necessary to "really valid study."[16] The classical and conventional library—the *temenos* with its silences, stacks, dusty chambers for reading, and *silenteum* caveat above the entrance—is nonetheless becoming discredited in most library circles.

In some libraries, notes Sallie Tisdale, NO SILENCE PLEASE signs are even posted as a part of library marketing campaigns.[17] Yet the library, "in a world that is growing increasingly raucous and cacophonous," is perhaps "the last outpost of silence and the quiet stir of thought, even as it is, the one surviving hope of intellectual freedom."[18]

If academic endeavors are about the creation and transfer of knowledge, then the role of concentration in the academic's life is of paramount importance. Psychologists have, for many years, recognized that high levels of stress and arousal (including noise and blinking lights) suppress attention processes.[19] But more is to be sought from the uniquely serene environment provided by a library, because more is to be sought from scholarship and study than the creation and transfer of knowledge. Perfect communication inside or outside academe has never and will never exist, no matter how inventive the assessment tool and regardless of our electronic aides. All humans know more than they can tell and "much of that which is known can never be shared." Silent atmospheres do support tangible forms of knowledge production, but they also make ascension from the world possible and allow for aloneness. Crossing to one's inner life, "resting in the self-same," is delightful, rejuvenating, instructive, and, consequently, a "part of the good life for everyone."[20]

In both Buddhist and Hindu traditions, a religious leader's ability to guide others in the community depends on silence being an integral part of his or her life. Bernard P. Dauenhauer in his book, *Silence*, writes:

> First, a muni is a person vowed to silence. But he is also "the capable one," the independent person, the one who achieves enlightenment without depending on a teacher. . . . And Buddas were said to help certain advanced disciples with a kind of silent power. Silence, then, is not only [an] ingredient in all dimensions of an enlightened person's individual life but also lies at the foundation of his capacity to lead others, to exercise influence in the community.[21]

Generally, worship by religious practitioners is carried out in temples. It is individual, rather than congregational.[22] Curtis Wright, who traces the functional origins of the library back to those Eastern sacral temples that housed the earliest written tablets, argues that these temple collections were "not devised for the busy practical people of Babylon in the mercenary hurly-burly of the market place." Nevertheless, these ancestral libraries—these buildings that were "specially designed for interpreting signs in the heavens"—existed for the public good:

> But if we want to think ourselves back into the skins of the people who created all of the civilized forms of government, we must lay aside our strong naturalistic presuppositions: they took the sacral temple seriously. . . . The temple was a place of revelation, "the one point on earth at which men could establish contact with other worlds. . . . " [It was] also . . . "a sort of antechamber between the worlds": once every year the king ascends from below as the god comes down from on high in order to meet in the holy of holies where revelation occurs, thus enabling the god and the king to correlate terrestrial with celestial affairs for the coming year.[23]

To be sure, the library has evolved structurally and philosophically since society emerged from the cradle of civilization. But the changes that have passed since the incorporation of the computer into library procedures—since the American Library Association's statement in 1978 that "all information must be available to all people in all formats purveyed through all communication channels and delivered at all levels of comprehension"—makes defining and implementing the relationship between education and "all information," terrestrial or otherwise, jarringly difficult.[24] In any case, most of us still call ourselves "librarians." And this name is still derived from a particular type of building. Librarianship remains—to a far greater degree than most others—a building-related profession.[25]

The archetypal, pre-twenty-first century librarian, who insisted on a patron's right to pursue his or her intellectual course undisturbed by distraction within the library building ("shhh!"), has been, every now and then, an object of ridicule in popular culture.[26] In an effort to erase this image from their twenty-first-century marketing plan, million-member trend-spotting associations of librarians seem bent on making today's library, in the words of Sallie Tisdale, "up-to-date, plugged in, and most definitely not set outside the ordinary day."[27] This trend is sad and insulting to public-library users, but it is an inexcusable affront to a generation of students (and their troubled communities) who utterly lack access to environments that are hospitable to serious meditation. As I pass through the corridors of my university library, I am both distressed and moved to see the study carrels and "quiet study areas" increasingly packed with students who, like endangered animals in a dried-up landscape, have instinctively sought out the last few watering holes of quiet thought.

"It is the right things about librarianship that are the least dramatic, the least amenable to spectacle," writes Jesse Shera.[28] William Wisner echoes this sentiment in his book *Whither the Postmodern Library*:

> I treasured all along the very marginality which so many others in the field found an embarrassing stereotype. . . . Patience, circumspection, steadfastness: these I felt were . . . the heroic values in a civilization.[29]

Wisner continues:

> I hate late-phase, unregulated capitalism. . . . And these same people have now invaded the library with a vengeance, with their understated suits and terrific haircuts and unstated contempt for anything that isn't a column with a total at the bottom. . . . Compared to their corporate fellows who live this game, we must have seemed easy pickings indeed. A little flattery and a slideshow can go a long way with people used to feeling marginal. . . . They sold us on speed, self-directedness and "efficiency"—that above all—and yet absolutely nothing in education is served by any of these values. In fact they are antithetical to education. And in the end, they are antithetical to reading. And it is in the singularly personal act of reading that any rebirth in an educational system as wigged out as ours must begin.[30]

The fact is, we still have not resolved the great philosophical question that underlies all librarianship: what is a book that a man may know it, and a man that he may know a book?"[31] And in this new accelerated vanishing point of illimitable information, we'd better crack the books and get thoughtful about this question if we are to do right by our students, faculty, staff, and each other. In our upward quest—obstructed more and more by raging haste, the lure of the stylish, the promise of mind-boggling access—we must never forget that the ultimate thing that any society, any university, produces is people. All other things are "intermediate goods." Economist Kenneth Boulding writes:

> No matter how rich we are or how powerful we are, if we do not produce people who can at least begin to expand into the enormous potential of man, the society must be adjudged a failure. The educational system is peculiarly specialized in the production of people, and it must never lose sight of the fact that it is producing people as ends, not as means. It is producing men not manpower, people, not biologically generated non-linear computers.[32]

Considering service to our academic communities is heady business and requires, in the words of Josef Pieper, a "willing immersion in, reality; an openness of the soul."[33] I am glad for the silent space to think upon this service, behind the heavy doors of my library.

Notes

1. Robert F. Goheen, *The Human Nature of a University* (Princeton, N.J.: Princeton University Press, 1969), 40.

2. Richard of Saint-Victor, *Selected Writings on Contemplation*, trans. Clare Kirchenberger (London: Faber and Faber, 1957), 122.

3. Adam Podgorecki, *Higher Faculties: A Cross-National Study of University Culture* (Westport, Conn.: Praeger, 1997), 129.

4. Goheen, *Human Nature*, 20, 33.

5. Corn Verhoven, *The Philosophy of Wonder*, trans. Mary Foran (New York: Macmillan, 1972), 184.

6. Sven Birkerts, *Readings* (St. Paul, Minn.: Graywolf, 1999), 67.

7. Podgorecki, *Higher Faculties*, 43.

8. Orrin E. Klapp, *Overload and Boredom: Essays on the Quality of Life in the Information Society* (New York: Greenwood Press, 1986), 28.

9. Center for Teaching and Learning, "The Bridge," February 10, 2002, at www.ctlt.wsu.edu/thebridge.asp.

10. Stephen Krashen, *The Power of Reading: Insights from the Research* (Englewood, Colo.: Libraries Unlimited, 1993), 37.

11. Patricia Broadfoot, "Editorial," *Assessment in Education: Principles, Policy & Practice*, 6(3) (1999), February 10, 2002, at search.epnet.com/direct.asp?an=2591865&db=afh.

12. Patricia Somers et al., "Faculty and Staff: The Weather Radar of Campus Climate," in *Campus Climate: Understanding the Critical Components of Today's Colleges and Universities,* ed. Karen W. Bauer (San Francisco: Jossey Bass, 1998), 40.

13. Christine A. Hult, *Researching and Writing in the Humanities and Arts* (Boston: Allyn & Bacon, 1996), 2–3.

14. Association of College and Research Libraries (ACRL), "Information Literacy Competency Standards for Higher Education" (Chicago: ACRL, 2000).

15. Jesse Shera, *The Compleat Librarian and Other Essays: Selections from the Columns Published in the Wilson Library Bulletin under the Title "Without Reserve"* (Cleveland: The Press of Case Western Reserve University, 1971), 175.

16. J. M. Orr, *Designing Library Buildings for Activity* (London: Andre Deutsch, 1972), 31.

17. Sallie Tisdale, "Silence, Please: The Public Library As Entertainment Center," *Harper's,* March 1997: 73.

18. Shera, *The Compleat Librarian,* 169.

19. Shirley Fisher, *Stress in Academic Life: The Mental Assembly Line* (Bristol, Pa.: The Society for Research into Higher Education and Open University Press, 1994), 13, 17.

20. Shera, *The Compleat Librarian,* 179, 175.

21. Bernard P. Dauenhauer, *Silence: The Phenomenon and Its Ontological Significance* (Bloomington: Indiana University Press, 1980), 110.

22. *Encyclopedia of Religion,* s. v. "temple."

23. Curtis H. Wright, *The Oral Antecedents of Greek Librarianship* (Provo, Utah: Brigham Young University Press, 1977), 55–58.

24. Tisdale, "Silence, Please," 68.

25. Michael J. Crosbie and Damon D. Hickey, *When Change Is Set in Stone: An Analysis of Seven Academic Libraries Designed by Perry Dean Rogers & Partners* (Chicago: Association of College and Research Libraries, 2001), 6.

26. Shera, *The Compleat Librarian,* 172.

27. Tisdale, "Silence, Please," 66.

28. Shera, *The Compleat Librarian,* 17.

29. William H. Wisner, *Whither the Postmodern Library: Libraries, Technology, and Education in the Information Age* (Jefferson, N.C.: McFarland, 2000), 107.

30. Wisner, *Whither the Postmodern Library,* 92–93.

31. Shera, *The Compleat Librarian,* 179.

32. Kenneth E. Boulding, *Beyond Economics: Essays on Society, Religion, and Ethics* (Ann Arbor: University of Michigan Press, 1968), 175.

33. Josef Pieper, *An Anthology* (San Francisco: Ignatius Press, 1989), 141.

Instead of planting our solitude with our own dream blossoms, we choke the space with continuous music, chatter and companionship to which we do not even listen. It is simply there to fill the vacuum. When the noise stops there is no inner music to take its place. We must re-learn to be alone.

—Anne Morrow Lindbergh, *Gift from the Sea*

CHAPTER THREE

Moving Beyond the "Re" Generation: Making Libraries and Librarians Count in the Twenty-first Century

Celia E. Rabinowitz

> The main function of the teacher is not to teach science, math, or literature; it is to make being an adult seem like a worthwhile option.
>
> —Mihaly Csikszentmihalyi

In ninety-nine years, when library school students are nearing the end of the twenty-first century (yes, Virginia, there will still be library schools), librarians from the end of the twentieth century are likely to be described as belonging to the "re" generation. That's because we have spent much of the last decade trying to figure out how to reconfigure, re-structure, reinvent, redefine, reposition, realign, and in the words of one of the century's greatest, get more R-E-S-P-E-C-T. No type of library has been immune. Academic librarians worry about becoming obsolete as a result of outsourcing, online databases, and the increasingly ubiquitous and popular full-text resources. Who will need us? How do we persuade faculty and administrators that we are still a relevant part of the academic mission and program of our institutions? Will anyone even come to the library anymore? "Why Don't More Faculty Love Librarians?" a recent article title lamented.[1] A search of Library Literature reveals that over 400 articles were published between 1990 and 2000 with the subject headings "college & university libraries" and "relations with faculty and curriculum." It was a hot topic to write about.

But what about these articles: "Selling the College Library's Services," "Are College Libraries Essential?" "The Place of the College Library in the Instructional Program"?[2] Written more than fifty years ago, these articles reveal concerns about the role of the academic library and librarians that are amazingly similar to those of the past decade. And those who despair that the library is no longer the heart of the academy should look carefully at Ernest Boyer's work on undergraduate education. It seems doubtful that the library ever was the blood-pumping vital organ that it has been portrayed to be.[3] Boyer's influential study found that around half of all undergraduates spent less than two hours per week in the library. He describes the library as a "neglected resource" but says that library staff is as "important to teaching as are classroom teachers." But again, this is not really news, since nearly fifty years before Boyer's study it had been observed that faculty members "are making only a very limited use of the library in their teaching work. [Students] do not use the library's books because in a great deal of their work they do not have to."[4]

The situation may not be as gloomy as it seems. Some of the changes in the past fifteen years have allowed libraries to take what Boyer identified as shortcomings and to turn them into opportunities to create new services that have enhanced the librarian's role on campus. For example, he noted that the library had, in many cases, become a glorified study hall.[5] And there has been a recent flurry of publication about the impact of electronic resources on library gate and circulation counts.[6] At my library, the addition of sixteen "lab" workstations, complete with an array of application software, has resulted in steadily increasingly higher head counts. While our campus computer lab is often half-empty, on most days almost every workstation in the library is full by 10 A.M., and we have counted fifty or sixty students in the building at 9 P.M. and 10 P.M., even during the first few weeks of the semester. And the students writing papers are also reading e-mail and magazines, looking at reference materials, asking the librarians for assistance, and enjoying the atmosphere that provides them with the best conditions for working (and yes, we have relaxed our policy on food and drink). Boyer and others may have actually underestimated the importance of the library as a physical space for all types of work, including group study, quiet reading, and writing papers (now done online instead of on a typewriter).

Despite the dangerously Rodney Dangerfield=like quality of our collective angst, the 1980s and 1990s produced ground-breaking advances in the creation of the information-literacy movement, as well as important research on faculty/librarian interaction, the impact of new formats on information production and access to those formats, and new organizational structures for libraries and computer centers. Publications that focus on praxis (outreach, new models for reference service, cataloging electronic resources) are eagerly sought, and listservs abound with requests for "how have you been doing it right?" advice.

And not all institutions have experienced the symptoms of obsolescence that seem so pervasive, at least according to the literature. At St. Mary's College of Maryland, a public honors liberal arts college with 1,600 students, and at other small residential institutions where the reference librarians are generalists who teach, do reference, coordinate collection development, manage electronic resources, arrange displays, and perform a variety of other public services, wired residence halls and online resources available 24/7 have not resulted in as great a reduction in circulation or reference statistics as seems to be the case in larger universities. Our electronic reserves service is incredibly popular among faculty and students, yet we still have a large number of traditional print reserves (and students in the library using them). And although we are still in the process of creating the kind of information-literacy program that we dream about, faculty ask us to teach, they understand their responsibility to attend instructional sessions, and they use the Web pages that we create. Most days I feel optimistic about our future (when I'm not rebooting computers or trying to persuade a student that a source we own in print may be better than the one in full-text online!).

The literature indicates that we have engaged in this kind of soul-searching before. So, is all of this preoccupation with reinventing ourselves and our libraries just another iteration in a cycle characterized by changing academic and intellectual values or by technological changes?

In what ways has the Internet radically changed the way we should think about what we do? And what about critical shifts in the direction of higher education? What values and foundational concepts remain constant throughout these periods of change and uncertainty? I suggest that we look at what we have learned from the literature of the 1990s, specifically about faculty and administration, what we know of our own institutions, and what we know about our professional values. We need to move into the new century with increased confidence in ourselves and our work and with less panic about our professional survival.

Faculty and Administration: Fear and Loathing on the Road to Respect

The Faculty

Larry Hardesty and Deborah Grimes have each written revealing studies of the academic librarian's potentially most important allies or most powerful critics.[7] Our pleas for respect are most often aimed at faculty, and our well-argued justifications for continued funding and staffing find themselves on the doorsteps of chief academic officers everywhere. And often what motivates us is the myth of the library as the heart and life-blood of the college.

Hardesty's award-winning study focused on fundamental differences between faculty and librarian cultures: faculty members are valued for what they know, while librarians are valued for the ways they help others learn. The very professional traits that we value (the ability to mediate between student and information resources and our role as generalists) lead faculty to devalue us in the eyes of faculty. Hardesty maintains that the burden is on librarians to learn to communicate effectively with faculty members because they often view us as subordinate. I think this explains our tendency of as librarians to place ourselves in the position of asking for permission when talking with faculty colleagues. For example, you might hear us asking, "Would you consider . . . ?" or "Would you allow me to . . . ?" rather than talking with faculty peers as colleagues who share a commitment to the same mission. Let's face it: not only do many faculty members not think of the library as the heart of the college, but we seem to be more like the kidneys—often ignored when we're around but missed when significantly compromised or removed.

Institution type and size can play significant roles in determining the "status" of librarians on a campus, regardless of other conditions, such as faculty rank and tenure. One of the advantages of the smaller college is the opportunity for librarians to be visible around campus to students, faculty, and administration in a variety of capacities (on committees, at campus cultural events, sponsoring student clubs, on the basketball court at lunch, teaching in academic programs, etc.). These activities and events often present opportunities for discussion, but most importantly, they are powerful evidence of our presence in the life of the institution. I am convinced that, regardless of institution size, the attitudes and actions of the librarians inside and outside the library have much more to do with how they (and the library) are viewed and valued than other factors, including formal faculty status or tenure.

Each of us has had his or her own experiences that illustrate Hardesty's thesis about cultural differences between faculty and librarians. We certainly collect plenty of anecdotal evidence every day. Here is an example from my campus: I ran into a faculty member in the locker room of the gym one day at lunch time as we were both getting dressed after exercising. She caught me off guard when she asked me if I was "done for the day." This professor is one of the most dedicated teachers I know (and a regular library user), but she seemed surprised when I reminded her that I am expected to be at work from 8 A.M. to 5 P.M. every day. How could a faculty member who is often seen in the library at all hours and on weekends be so unaware of the working routines of the librarians?

A recent post on the bibliographic-instruction listserv (BI-L) created a flurry of responses and provides another illustration. An instruction librarian recounts an experience in a class when an instructor not only sat in the back grading papers, but also listened to, and reported the score of, a major major-league baseball game. This librarian remarked in her post that she decided it was not her place to say anything to the instructor, since she was glad that he had brought his class in at all.[8]

How do we take situations like these and capitalize on them instead of becoming defensive, hostile, or even worse, resigned?

The Administration

Deborah Grimes's study of the ways university administrators view their libraries and librarians directly challenges the image of the library as heart of the academy. Unstable funding, lack of access to top institutional administrators, and a poor understanding of the contribution of the academic library and its librarians to the mission of the institution have resulted in a subordinate status for the library on many campuses. I think Grimes's research is most valuable for what the survey results reveal about the attitudes and beliefs of many administrators. And I think we should take advantage of the opportunities this knowledge gives us to formulate new strategies.

Grimes, focusing on the concept of "library centrality," asked administrators at five large universities what that term meant to them. And even at St. Mary's, some of the perceptions and attitudes about the library that Grimes found at larger institutions seem to be prevalent among both administrators and faculty. Thus, during a recent project to rewrite the faculty by-laws a faculty member explained a proposed change by suggesting that the librarian of the college probably had "better things to do" than to serve as a permanent (although ex officio) member of the Curriculum Committee. The proposed change was eventually withdrawn before it could come up for a vote.

What Grimes found is that most of the administrators in her study did not think of library centrality as any of the following:

- Innovation by librarians (except when related to information technology)
- Collaboration between librarians and faculty
- Participation in committee structure
- Acquisition of outside funding
- Campus visibility (they recognized the visibility of the library building but not the librarians)

On the other hand, the following aspects of the library were identified as illustrating or embodying centrality:

- Resources (size of collection, quality of information storage and retrieval, facilities, etc.)
- Personnel (quality of staff, service attitude)
- Prestige (faculty and student opinion of the library, comparative statistics, etc.)

These Chief Academic Officers (CAOs) and Chief Information Officers (CIOs) somehow do not make the connection between the resources and prestige they value and the role of librarians, through innovation and collaboration, to manage and teach the use of resources, and thus to contribute to creating prestige. The library is seen as central to the institutional mission, but the librarians are not.

Now What?

Perhaps the picture looks pretty bleak. Just as the institutions in which we work have been challenged by the growth of distance learning, preoccupation with the "wired" (and wireless) campus, and fluctuating enrollments, libraries have been challenged by these same factors, as well as by radical changes that have evolved in just the past decade in the forms of and manner of accessing information. These changes include online database and full-text access (which have been challenges for our colleagues in acquisitions and cataloging, too); shifting curricula (more collaborative and research work for students, focus on assessment and clearly articulated learning outcomes at all levels, and changes made in anticipation of, or in response to, accreditation visits); the addition of lab workstations and wireless computing in libraries (in my library we began loaning wireless laptops from our circulation services during the fall 2001 semester); efforts to focus on integrating information-literacy competency standards (and often technology competencies) into the curriculum; some reported declining circulation statistics, longer reference interactions, and more uncertainty about funding and maintaining collection levels of all sorts, just to name a few.

Perhaps it is no wonder that we feel compelled to rethink most of the ways that we have done our work in the past. And this kind of reassessment can be very beneficial. It is crucial that we be willing to try new services, procedures, staffing patterns, or policies. But I think it is also helpful to remember that this same kind of assessment has happened before during the history of academic librarianship. And some of our more recent efforts at rethinking have begun to appear almost desperate. We have created an entire category of published literature that focuses on new models, new structures, and new services. This literature seems predicated on the assumption that we are doomed to become redundant and obsolete if we do not make radical changes in the way we work. But these changes also need to be based on some core principals that serve to provide both foundation and continuity. One of the great values of studies like the ones Hardesty and Grimes undertook is that they remind us that we have work to do. We have to earn and demand respect and a place at the table. One of the ways we do that is by acknowledging, and not abandoning, what we know we do well.

What's a Librarian to Do?

While preparing for a talk I gave to the South Carolina Library Association Academic Library Section in 1999, I ran across an article called "Adaptive and Maladaptive Narcissism among University Faculty, Clergy, Politicians, and Librarians."[9] Using popular stereotypes, the authors surveyed these groups to assess levels of adaptive narcissism (the good kind, characterized by friendliness, sociability, and warmth), and maladaptive narcissism (the bad kind, characterized by ambition, acquisitiveness, and domineering behavior). It turns out that librarians did not score significantly high or low on either scale (yes, it's true, politicians scored highest in total narcissism). But librarians (who as a group were identified as having less of a need for prestige, social attention, power, and admiration from others!) did score the lowest of all groups on the leadership/authority scale.

With those findings in mind, I offer this set of suggestions for establishing our identity and place on campus as we move into the next century of academic librarianship.

- *Figure out what counts.* Try to decide what matters most at any particular time and for the long haul. Is it funding for a new database, a change in policy, the introduction of a new service, implementing information-literacy initiatives? What are you passionate about? The things that make you passionate about your work will be easy for you to talk about, and your enthusiasm will be apparent to those faculty and administrators with whom you come into contact.
- *Don't ask permission.* Take the initiative in engaging faculty in collaborative projects (e.g., removing print/online journal overlaps or assessing materials for withdrawal). Supply suggestions, ask for feedback, but provide clear deadlines and take action. Ask for specific examples when faculty or administrators complain (or pass along

complaints). Establish your expertise. For example, when a faculty member dismisses a suggested resource for purchase as too general, take the opportunity to remind her about our standards and broad view of collection development in supporting the entire mission of the college not just the needs of one department. Inform faculty that your policy requires the attendance of faculty at instruction sessions and find opportunities to help faculty learn how they can contribute to the learning outcomes of that session.

- *Talk the talk.* When you tell faculty colleagues that you have a class to teach, and their response is to look surprised and comment that they did not know you taught, resist the temptation to say, "It's only a library-instruction session." Make faculty aware of prep time you need for classes; know the curriculum and engage faculty in discussions about it; use your knowledge of faculty culture to draw faculty and administrators into conversation about library-related matters.

- *Be accommodating, but not subservient.* Facilitate rush orders for materials or requests for classes on short notice when it makes sense but clarify the circumstances and make expectations clear. Otherwise, you devalue your own time, and others will, too.

- *Work WITH it, not against it.* Try not to compete with initiatives in information technology. This is becoming increasingly challenging as more funds are allocated to technology and as many (especially administrators) see the library as little more than the technology that keeps it running. Faculty can be our allies here—most have something to say about students' unsophisticated reliance on electronic resources. Find a way to work with instructional technologists and with your colleagues at the technology help desk.

- *Ask the hard questions, but be ready to compromise.* Don't be afraid to challenge faculty and administrators. If you are asked for a new resource, request information about thoughtful plans for introducing students to that resource. If you are asked to implement a new service, put together a detailed (but not antagonistic) document outlining the impact on staffing, materials, and budget. But also be willing to compromise when the long-term payoff may be to your benefit.

- *Capitalize on your strengths and learn what matters.* Highlight your strengths—convenient open hours (prospective students are surprised to learn that we are open until midnight five nights a week), remote access, location (my library has spectacular views of the college waterfront), new resources. Make sure people know about them. Don't underestimate the ability of students to provide support. Be aware of curricular or governance issues that might affect you and don't be reluctant to get involved however you can. Knowledge really is power. Stay on top of the literature in higher education. Consider reading or skimming regularly *The Chronicle of Higher Education, Change, College Teaching, Educause Review, Feminist Teacher,* and the like.

One of the greatest strengths of academic librarians is the global institutional view that we have. We often know what is happening in classrooms, in the computing center, and in some administrative office (especially if you are on the receiving end of requests for information from those offices!). Our job is to look broadly and to advocate for a wide range of interests and needs. We need to remind our campus colleagues of how important that is. It is a source of strength, not weakness. And we need to remind ourselves. Even as we struggle to think about and learn how we will evolve as new forms and types of information arrive at our doorsteps, we should move forward with confidence. What will make the reconfiguring, restructuring, repositioning, reinventing, redefining, and realigning successful is the continuity that reminds our student, faculty, and administrative community of who we are. That familiarity and recommitment to our fundamental role and mission will help us maintain our sanity and continue to garner the respect that we deserve.

Notes

1. William F. Birdsall, "Why Don't More Faculty Love Librarians?" *Journal of Academic Librarianship* 17 (1999): 339–67.

2. Katharine M. Stokes, "Selling the College Library's Services," *College and Research Libraries* 4 (March 1943): 120–27; Floyd E. Orton, "Are College Libraries Essential?" *Library Journal* 75 (August 1950): 1269, 1326; W. Stanley Hoole, "The Place of the College Library," *Journal of Higher Education* 14 (1943): 370–73, September 1, 2001, at JSTOR http://www.jstor.org.

3. Ernest L. Boyer, *College: The Undergraduate Experience in America* (New York: Harper & Row, 1987), 160, 164.

4. Bennett Harvie Branscomb, *Teaching with Books: A Study of College Libraries* (Hamden, Conn.: Shoe String Press, 1964), 52.

5. Boyer, *College*, 161.

6. Scott Carlson, "The Deserted Library," *Chronicle of Higher Education* 16 (November 2001), November 9, 2001, at www.chronicle.com/free.

7. Larry Hardesty, "Faculty Culture and Bibliographic Instruction: An Exploratory Analysis," *Library Trends* 44 (1995): 339–67; Deborah J. Grimes, *Academic Library Centrality: User Success through Service, Access, and Tradition*, ACRL Publications in Librarianship 50 (Chicago: ACRL, 1998).

8. Caroline M. Bordinaro, "Instructor Behavior During BI's," post to Bibliographic Instruction Listserv, October 18, 2001, at bi-l@listserv.byu.edu.

9. Robert W. Hill and Gregory P. Yousey, "Adaptive and Maladaptive Narcissism among University Faculty, Clergy, Politicians, and Librarians," *Current Psychology* 17 (1999): 163, September 9, 1999, at EbscoHost Academic Search Elite at www.ehost.epnet.com.

It would be too pat, perhaps, to say that modern people, men and women, expect the unexpected. But they certainly expect, or are inured to, constant change. . . . Unquestionably, people sense constant movement, change, alteration, and "progress." Even clothes are supposed to change from year to year: there is this year's fashion, and last year's fashion, and the fashions of the year before.

Then there is the idea of "news," that is, of something novel happening every day, something worth reporting. Millions of people wake up in the morning and watch the news on television; they may also listen to radio news throughout the day and later catch the evening television news. It would be unthinkable to read in the newspapers or to hear on television that "nothing much happened today." There is always news, always something going on, always change. Some days bring major headlines; other days are quieter. But there is never no news: the message we get every day is that things are never exactly the same.

—Lawrence M. Friedman, *The Horizontal Society*

CHAPTER FOUR

Reference Librarians
As Wild Animals

David Isaacson

Twenty-two acknowledged concubines and a library of sixty-two
thousand volumes, attested to the variety of his inclinations; and
from the productions which he left behind him, it appears that
the former as well as the latter were designed for use rather than
ostentation.

—Edward Gibbon (1737–1794), *The Decline and Fall of the*
Roman Empire, a comment on Gordian the Younger,
a wealthy Roman

If Gordian the Younger ever needed to talk about books (or concubines) with a reference librarian, that public servant could not be the
domesticated variety. Gordian would need to meet Monty Python.
"You see, I don't believe that libraries should be drab places where people sit in silence, and that's been the main reason for our policy of em-
ploying wild animals as librarians."[1] Monty Python was talking about

one of my fantasy images of reference librarians when he made this observation. Like Superman masquerading as the mild-mannered Clark Kent, I am a very different person just beneath my quiet reference-librarian exterior. I am really a wild animal—a beast. Most frequently I am a gorilla or a lion. I prefer to be a lion because gorillas are sometimes mistaken for ordinary librarians, and I know that I am not ordinary. My real self wants to stalk prey in the book stacks, yowl imprecations over the intercom, and lick my whelps (either colleagues or patrons) into shape. So, when offered the job of chief reference librarian, I pounced on it.

I don't mean to harm anyone by my beastly behavior, but here's one mousy librarian who is better typecast as a lion. Some of this fantasy is probably over-compensation, like the character Conan the Librarian.[2] Just as Rodney Dangerfield groused about "getting no respect," some of us librarians have had it with the stereotype of the lady with pursed lips, a pencil sticking out of the bun in her hair, compulsively insisting on order in her book stacks, among her paperclips, and now, within her databases as well. Lots of things are wrong with this image. For one thing, there are male as well as female librarians.[3] But it isn't sex or gender that determines who librarians are. We are concerned with order—we have to be—but some of us aren't compulsive about it. Which brings me back to wild animals.

If librarians are wild animals, they act by instinct as much as by conscious thought. My instinct as a librarian is to follow the five basic laws of librarianship promulgated by the venerable S. R. Ranganathan:

1. Books are for use.
2. Every reader has his or her book.
3. Every book has its reader.
4. Save the time of the reader.
5. The library is a growing organism.

Acting according to these instincts, I want to do everything I can to bring library patrons and resources together. I substitute the word "resources" for "books" because the information we provide our users comes packaged in many other forms besides old-fashioned books. But as soon as I've uttered the word "information," I want to modify it. I don't believe librarians are merely in the mere information-exchange business. One of our jobs is to provide sources of information to people, but it's very difficult to know whether our users are truly informed as a result. Our instinct as librarians is to help users become learners. Rather than merely providing potential data and information, many of us want to help people actually give specific form to facts, data, and bits and bytes of information. We shouldn't be viewing patrons as simply being "filled in" by information—as if they were passive and empty vessels. Librarians and patrons should be actively creating these vessels together. Becoming informed is often an ongoing process, rather than a done deal. We make forms of information, rather than becoming simply becoming informed. Like artists, we create shapes—forms that vary according to the person asking us a question but also forms that vary because of how we choose to define the "information packages" we create with, as well as for, the patron.

Beastly librarians should seek to teach users how to be proficient hunters of information. We should teach information proficiency, not information literacy (IL). Originally, before it became such a loose metaphor, "literacy" meant the ability to read. But, that is all the word connoted. Literacy simply means the ability to decode writing. A literate person isn't necessarily informed about anything. A merely literate person may not be very good at reading, or very interested in it. Laura Bush, former school librarian and now First Lady, has been an outspoken opponent of "aliteracy," descriptive of people who can read but for various reasons choose not to. Many people don't read with pleasure, understanding, or curiosity. Sadly, it is also true that reference and instruction librarians encounter many "information literate" people who are similarly alienated from the fun and value of real information seeking. There is some value in substituting the word "competency" for "literacy," because competency suggests the ability to find information not just the ability to decode it. I would rather that librarians teach people to be competent rather than merely literate. But I think "proficiency" is a better choice than either "literacy" or "competency" because it comes right out and says that someone is good at something. That is what we want to do, isn't it—to make patrons proficient in finding information sources?

To make patrons proficient, we should not passively wait for them to ask us questions. Nor should we shush them. Just the opposite: we need to be bold, brave, and uncommonly active. If the librarian is a wild an-imal, he or she isn't, by definition, domesticated. No one takes care of wild animals. They hunt for themselves. In a library that has gone back to nature, we would dispense with the mere veneer of civilization. We would not stand on ceremony. We would actively engage our patrons in talk. Instead of being passively on call, ready to interpret citations and explore indexes when asked, we would talk, often in the most animated fashion, with our users. They wouldn't look for us; we would stalk them.[4]

Do not imagine that the wild beast wants to devour the library user; rather, his mission is to help the user learn to hunt. My image of the reference librarian as wild animal is something like that of Simba's fa-ther in *The Lion King*. Mufasa teaches Simba to fight for himself be-cause he knows that one day the son must succeed him. Few of our users—of whatever age—are really self-sufficient learners. They may not know it, but they need our help. Out of pride or ignorance, these users don't always feel that they can ask us for help. In the Monty Python library, our users don't have to ask for help. Librarians provide help without being sought out. The librarian lives where the wild things are. Scary at first, but what else do you expect from the jungle?

I don't mean to suggest that the librarian is always an in-your-face presence. But she is mistress of all she surveys. The merely domesti-cated librarian only follows narrow rules. The wild librarian knows when to break rules and when to combine the verbal and logical habits of the left side of the brain with the associative, more visual habits of the right side of the brain. Beastly librarians take risks all the time. They free-associate as much as they deduce. They make it virtually im-possible for the user to follow only the straight and narrow.

Wild librarians make good World Wide Web searchers. The Web has facilitated wild behavior both among librarians and users. At its worst, the Web merely reinforces freaky, impulsive surfing from one website to another. This kind of wildness may be fun, but it wastes energy. At its best, the Web makes it easier not only to authenticate facts but to think creatively. The trick is to balance the left and right sides of the brain, reason and intuition, words and images, deduction and induction, re-straint and wildness. A successful beast does not merely roam around hoping to find food. A lion has marked his territory, defended it against rivals, and knows when, where, and how to hunt game.

Similarly, a librarian doesn't only act on instinct. These instincts are focused, developed, and conditioned. The mother lion not only suckles her pride, she picks her cubs up by the scruffs of their necks and bats and cuffs them. She patiently shows them how to defend themselves against predators. But she also, in turn, shows them how to become predators themselves. The cubs play with one another to learn how to fend for themselves but also to learn how to hunt in a pack. This is equivalent to library students getting basic training in library school. But much of our learning takes place on the job. Some of it is mere training—learning cataloging rules and basic reference sources is fairly tame stuff. But the wild librarian knows when to lie motionlessly in wait, when to pounce, and how to use both claws and teeth. If she doesn't learn these skills, she will not survive.[5]

And the wild librarian hunts by feel as well as by memory and training. The super-sensitive sense of smell in lions is like that extra sense some veteran reference librarians possess to track down elusive answers to questions that overly rule-bound librarians don't know how to answer. The polite name for this extra-rational quality is "discretion"; but let's not pussyfoot—let's be lion-like and call this quality "cunning." Some of the most cunning work we do comes from the one-on-one personal, intuitive, and nonverbal relationships we develop with users, which complement the rational and logical work of decoding the words of a question.

The wild librarian is not afraid to engage a user in a spirited conversation. Tame librarians, on the other hand, not only hush their patrons, but even worse, they hush themselves. It is very ironic and deeply unprofessional for academic librarians, traditionally among the strongest defenders of free speech as well as the academic freedom that enlarges upon our Constitutional guarantee of free speech, to muzzle themselves. Nothing is more depressing to a wild librarian than the demeaning spectacle of a cowardly lion colleague, afraid of her own shadow. Reference librarians who merely answer the questions patrons ask, instead of poking around to find out what they actually mean, are not doing their jobs very well. There must be a give-and-take between patron and librarian. If the librarian is only polite and decorous, the patron is not likely to reveal the full context of those hard questions that require negotiation. We have no need for mousy reference librarians.[6]

The best environment for a wild librarian to work in, accordingly, is an open space. Yes, there should be closed, quiet areas for traditional private study. For those patrons who need extra privacy, carrels providing isolation ought to be provided. Some library study is contemplative. Some students want only to commune with texts, databases, or microfilm, not with live human beings. But groups of students—with or without a professor or librarian acting as a teacher—also need study rooms where they can talk without disturbing the patrons who do need and deserve quiet.

Unlike study areas, the reference area ought to be buzzing with activity. Librarians actively involved in reference and instruction work (especially in academic libraries where the main purpose is teaching students and faculty how to use library resources) need to be vocal.[7] Real teaching librarians may need to do more than simply talk with patrons. Contrary to the standard expectations of merely polite behavior, I want to make a case for librarians who are prepared to argue—sometimes fervently—with patrons. Teaching is not only imparting information. That is the least important role public-service librarians perform. When librarians actually teach patrons how to engage in a "conversation" with a complex reference book or database, they need time to explain, revise, question, and reformulate.

Librarians and their patrons have different learning and teaching styles. Whether we are teaching one-on-one at the reference desk, to a group in a wired classroom, in an informal tutorial in the reference stacks, or at a group of computer terminals, we need time, space, and freedom to explore ideas.

Real teaching and learning are not tame exercises at all. It may not require lions or gorillas, but real learning sometimes necessitates guerilla action. Some learning is subversive in the very best sense of that word. Real learning subverts conventional expectations. Real learning—which beastly librarians are eminently qualified to encourage—is a slow, sometimes painful (as well as pleasurable) process. It seldom proceeds in a straight line. It is certainly not always hierarchical. Real learning is exciting. Like hunting, real learning requires trial and error. It requires us to be wild. Not wild in the sense of unrestrained and wholly unpredictable behavior but wild in the sense of basic, primordial openness to experience. Socrates was a bit of a beast as he walked around Athens asking probing questions. We could do worse than to hire Socratic librarians to roam the library asking questions that make our patrons think. So what if these questions disturb some of them? Education should disturb and unsettle fixed beliefs.

Real learning is emotional as well as intellectual. The hunt itself is as fulfilling as the goal. Far from being a chore, library research can be an adventure in critical thinking. Wild librarians impart some of this joy of hunting through their example. If necessary, they may even impose their will on lazy, recalcitrant, or inattentive students. Real teachers are proud of the mastery of their craft. There should not be an even exchange between teacher and student. Of course, teachers also learn from students, but students come to teachers because they trust us to guide them. If we really are teachers, we ought to know something students don't know. What we know may relate to something innate within students or something external to them. No one is born knowing the Library of Congress (LC) Classification System, but we human beings seem to be genetically predisposed to want order in our lives. The Dewey Decimal System and LC are attempts by librarians to tidy up a messy intellectual world.

Sometimes the best teacher is a sage on the stage, sometimes a guide on the side. The librarian teacher may need to be both. In either case, real teachers are not merely polite. I don't mean to insist that teachers should be confrontational. Some teachers are successful by aping apes, but this isn't what I mean by wildness. Sure, some of the questions we answer at reference desks and in classrooms require nothing more than formulaic responses. Veteran librarians can be easily bored by such questions. We might prefer to have robots answer these mere mechanics-of-use questions, the humdrum directionals, the monotonous one-step look-ups, the queries that computers were supposed to save human beings from having to answer. The trick with these questions is to focus on the individual as much as on the question. Though an old one for us, it is a new experience for the patron. We should show these patrons that, even if the question is old hat to us, each of them is wearing a unique chapeau.

The adventure and challenge of the hunt—where wild, rather than tame, librarians are needed—comes with the meatier questions, the ones that don't have pat answers, those that can't be answered "yes" or "no," but require a "maybe," and "but," and "by the way." The librarian who is used to operating in the wild lives for these more substantial questions. He is not afraid to question the questioner, not giving him the third degree, but not using kid gloves either. Students and faculty members unacquainted with library resources know when a librarian is only acting as an authority and when she wants to engage them in that wonderful dialog that sometimes sends shivers up and down the spines of teachers and learners.

As a beastly reference librarian, I don't have to personally stalk prey to be a successful hunter-teacher. Some of the most successful teaching a librarian can do is virtual, if not also virtuous. The way we design Web pages and the way we respond to e-mail reference questions is becoming as important as, and sometimes more important than, how we conduct ourselves in the strictly "live" mode. We need to be as open to change and innovation in our virtual incarnations as we are in person at the reference desk or in the classroom.

Untamed reference librarians need human interactions in order to do their best work. Ironically, live-chat reference services may turn out to be livelier than some of the encounters with reluctant users who actually appear in the flesh at the reference desk. I would rather teach a motivated user on e-mail or over the telephone than an unmotivated one who slinks up to the reference desk with an attitude, presenting himself in the library only because his teacher requires it. It is also ironic that some of our most remote users may be only a few feet away from the reference desk. If the patron does not ask a question, how do we know he doesn't know what he's doing?

The beastly librarian roams around asking people if they are finding what they want. She doesn't always wait, passively, to be asked for help. More and more library patrons seem to be quite content working alone at computer terminals. Actually, more and more librarians are also happy as clams interacting with terminals for hours at a time. Many people seem to prefer e-mail to actual conversation. Somehow, a conversation on a cell phone, for many people, takes priority over a conversation in person. I would like to see reference librarians offer an alternative to the alluring, but sometimes illusive, companionship of digital interfaces. However wedded most of us are to our electronic devices, they are only extensions of ourselves, means of communication, not ends in themselves.

If you don't like my extended metaphor of beastly reference librarians, I won't insist on it. My central point is a very old one, but one we sometimes forget. Academic libraries are not just repositories of information. Books and databases are inert things until people activate them. Librarians do have to quietly "tame" these resources by keeping them in order. Sometimes we have to tame unruly patrons, too. But in the best sense, academic reference librarians especially need to question the mere proprieties, the unquestioned conventions, the stale, box-like image of libraries as nothing more than quiet places of study.

I would much rather hire a real gorilla as a librarian than a fake one.

Notes

1. I found the transcript of this Monty Python episode on the Web at www.ibras.dk/montypython/episode10.htm#9. It is too long to include verbatim here, but the reader ought to know, in the interest of accurate bibliographic notation, that in this skit a vicar and a chairman interview Mr. Phipps, a man dressed as a gorilla, for a job as a librarian. The chairman notes that a gorilla might not be qualified for running a library because he would tend to frighten people. But this is just a ruse to see if Mr. Phipps is actually a gorilla. There follows an argument among the vicar, chairman, and Mr. Phipps about whether he really is a gorilla. When Mr. Phipps finally admits he is only posing as a gorilla, the job interview is ended: only real gorillas are qualified for the job as a librarian. The same reasoning applies to the lion-librarian interface.

2. There is a considerable dispute about the origin of the character of Conan the Librarian. Please follow this closely, because part of my argument about library beastliness hinges on the accurate tracing of the origin of this metaphor. *Worldcat* notes a fourteen-page book, published in 1985: *Conan, the Librarian: Everything You Wanted to Know about the DNR Library, but Didn't Know You Could Ask*. Written by Amir Zaman and Patricia Parsons and published by the Wisconsin Department of Natural Resources Library, this book is actually a public document, with the GovDoc number Nat 6/2:L 45/1985. But something is amiss. A Web search under "Conan Librarian" in Google on July 12, 2001, gives an entirely different perspective on the origin of this character and his subsequent avatars. According to www.aallnet.org/chapter/mall/conan/conanhp.html, Conan is a parody of Robert E. Howard's character, Conan the Barbarian, and first appeared in 1987 in a skit performed by the library staff at the William Mitchell College of Law talent show. However, these adventures are not available electronically and the designers of this Web page do not provide a bibliographic citation to a printed script. They do, however, provide a number of links to the Web adventures of Conan the Librarian. Conan

the Librarian should also be distinguished from an apparent avatar, Biblia, the Warrior Librarian, who has the habit of chewing out recalcitrant patrons in Latin. For instance, she might say to a patron who offers lame excuses about a damaged book, "Re vera, cara mea, mea nil refert," freely translated as "Frankly, my dear, I don't give a damn." For more of Biblia's Latin retorts see www.geocities.com/bibliophist/HUMOUR/latin.html.

At any rate, despite the uncertain origin of Conan the Librarian, I believe that he is of the same lineage as Monty Python's beastly librarian. He is also, clearly, a Jungian archetype. Some may quibble that beasts and barbarians really should be distinguished from one another, but this is a distinction without a difference as far as I am concerned. The beastly librarians I know are often taken for barbarians and vice versa. Q.E.D.

3. And I have it on good authority that both sexes, as well as numerous gender roles, can be beastly. Readers should be careful to note that my argument is nonsexist: both male and female librarians can, and indeed should, actually become wild beasts, not simply pretend to be them, as the unfortunate Mr. Phipps did.

4. It is clear that a library beast is carnivorous. While libraries have traditionally welcomed browsers and grazers, the librarian as gorilla, lion, or barbarian is no vegetarian. He or she must have real intellectual meat in order to survive, let alone prosper.

5. Even independent information brokers know they live in a highly competitive world. Academic librarians are by no means immune from the alluring dazzle of the commercial world. Besides, being made of ivory, the Ivory Tower has been constructed from the tusks and limbs of now endangered wild species, like elephants and whales.

6. The only exception would be mice that roar.

7. The author of this article has actually been shushed by a student for talking too loudly in the reference area. Talk about role reversal! He told this student to move on to a quiet area.

Where there is much desire to learn, there of necessity will be much arguing, many opinions; for opinion in good men is but knowledge in the making.

—John Milton

CHAPTER FIVE

Place and Space: Libraries and the Cartography of Knowledge

Barbara Fister

> The whole idea of a library is based on a misunderstanding: that a reader goes to the library to find a book whose title he knows. . . . The essential function of a library is to discover books of whose existence the reader had no idea.
>
> —Umberto Eco

Virtual libraries are nothing new. I've had one of my own for decades. My virtual library is not a clean or well-lighted place. Its ceilings are low, the stacks a claustrophobic maze. The dim and sputtering florescent lights shed stingy light through the mysterious tunnels of books. There's an odd corner where a tall, arched window has panes of glass so old that the bubbles trapped in it hold hundred-year-old air. The wavy striations in the glass warp the campus outside, where the trees forever wear autumn colors. In front of the window, there is a long wooden table, scarred over the years, carrying the idly inked initials of long-gone students and their profane expressions of existential angst. I have claimed it like a settler, marking my possession with a pile of books and papers, and, having claimed it, I make forays into the stacks between bouts of reading, daydreaming, and doodling. A blank notebook lies open; beside it, a Mont Blanc fountain pen that I lost some thirty years ago.

> The dingy, overcrowded university library where I spent countless undergraduate hours is only a memory now, replaced a few years ago by one that is airy and bright and full of computers. Although the wavy window glass is gone, students attending my alma mater can still can claim some personal corner near a window, assemble their books and printouts, set up their laptops, and daydream while watching the leaves turn color outside. It will leave its imprint in their memory and become their virtual library. At least I hope so.

My understanding of the world of ideas—and my sense that it is a mappable world, where communities can be located and distances traversed rather, than an inchoate, boundless void—has been shaped by exposure to a real library. I have a sense that texts in proximity (physically because of their arrangement on the shelves, virtually because of the connectedness of the ideas they engage) are communities in discourse that relate to one another in a conversational space that gets lost, somehow, in the impulsivity of following links from server to server—each ghostly page reordering pixels of light to present something new while extinguishing its predecessor. Because I have wandered through physical stacks, seen connections, and observed how books on the "same" subject can approach it so differently, I have the rough outlines of a map of what I know and what I have yet to discover. And where the map fades out into areas that are truly terra incognita, I have developed through familiarity with a physical library a sense of direction, a feel for the cardinal points, which I can use as I explore new lands.

The promise of virtual reality was heady stuff not long ago. We could invent and replay any experience we wanted, as many times as we wanted, and nobody got hurt. No longer slaves to linear thinking, we could create our own meaning by charting a course of our own devising through texts. Reading would become interactive. Texts would be claimed and reinvented by readers, who would become authors as they reinscribed the text with their own ordering principles. At the same time, gatekeepers in the form of editors and publishers would lose their power to authorize certain texts as valid—and exclude others from being heard at all. The author is dead; long live the author.[1]

One of the great promises of this virtual new world was that it would give us enormous freedom. We would not be subject to hierarchy or someone else's idea of the natural order. We would make our own meaning. This decentering of authority—and, at the same time, of the idea of order found in a library with its rules and categories and implied Great Chain of Being—would topple the tyranny of the expert and make us all equal. No more gatekeepers, those arbitrary arbiters of taste and quality. The virtual library is hip to the postmodernist condition: meaning is a slippery business; a text is not a text but a multitude of possibilities, depending on how it is read; order is an arbitrary construct understood best through deconstruction. No wonder Gertrude Himmelfarb, alarmed by the leveling effect of the Web, believed the Internet, and the revolution it was causing in the library, was going to finish the job of destroying culture that Jacques Derrida and his evil minions had started.[2]

But is this decentered realm of knowledge, where texts can be changed by reading them differently, really any different from the prelapsarian "real" library full of "real" books? How can anyone claim that reading, in the past, was anything but interactive? How can printed texts be faulted for being linear when I, as a reader, can flip the pages backwards or read them out of order? What is a hyperlink, after all, if not simply a faster footnote? And, as Tom Mann has pointed out, hasn't pulling books off the shelf and skimming their indexes and tables of contents and the first paragraphs of chapters always been a kind of full-text search?[3]

Years ago, Jorge Luis Borges described the universe as a "Library of Babel" that embraces a frighteningly vast space that has no center and no circumference.[4] It is a maze of an indeterminate number of interconnected hexagonal galleries full of an infinite number of books, all of which are unique—though many are imperfect copies of one another. The vastness of this library causes exhilaration and despair: "When it was announced that the Library contained all books, the first reaction was unbounded joy," the narrator tells us early in the story, but adds later "that unbridled hopefulness was succeeded, naturally enough, by a similarly disproportionate depression." Finding books in this library is a process of regression that mimics the slippage of meaning: "To locate book A, first consult book B, which tells where book A can be found; to locate book B, consult book C, and so on, into infinity." From this fruitless activity comes a deep sense of hopelessness: "It is in ventures such as these that I have squandered and spent my years."[5]

Though Borges published this story in 1941, he could have been describing the Web. Like the Library of Babel, the Web has no center. It is full of imperfect copies. And certainly many of us haves squandered our time seeking an ever-elusive idea through the regression of hyperlinks. Like Borges's library, what seems at first a wonderful and rich abundance of knowledge becomes a source of despair for the same reason: "The certainty that some bookshelf in some hexagon contained precious books, yet those precious books were forever out of reach, was almost unbearable."[6]

Of course, graduate students over the years have experienced the same sense of existential despair within the walls of a research library. The difference is, an academic library does have a center, it does have a circumference, and its walls contain not all knowledge but a limited amount that has been selected for a particular community of knowers. It is, by its very nature, a place to start. Students new to research can situate themselves in relation to what they do not yet know and gain the confidence that there is a way to find out.

In an early evocation of the virtual future, a 1995 television advertisement for MCI promised that the Internet "will connect all points. . . . It will not go from here to there. There will be no there. We will all only be here."[7] This is a strangely evocative of the formless, decentered, urban nowhere that Gertrude Stein found in Oakland, California—a place where, famously, "there is no there there." This brave new world of cyberspace promises to banish "there" and be instead a limitless sprawl in which the gang's all here—but what can "here" possibly mean when it embraces everywhere?

Libraries have a fairly simple solution to that dilemma. Here we have literature, there you'll find art. Upstairs is physics and nearby chemistry. Within these categories, we sort things even further so that on the shelves holding physics books we can find those that focus on solid state physics. With just a bit of a wander to one side, we're in fluid mechanics. And when a new idea comes along—say, computers, or communication studies, or chaos theory—we'll find a way of squeezing the new in among the old.

Libraries are not closed systems. They offer taxonomies of knowledge, not to fix what is or what should be but to be deliberately permeable. The order of libraries is a means of allowing very different ideas to find each other and have a good brawl. The order only exists to be destabilized.

Or as Alberto Manguel puts it, "A room determined by artificial categories, such as a library, suggests a logical universe, a nursery universe in which everything has its place and is defined by it."[8] These categories are not fixed or particularly meaningful in and of themselves—they're simply a way of mapping knowledge that is not static, but boundless and always changing. They invite dissent by bringing together texts that interpret things differently and which will, in turn, be interpreted differently by different readers:

> The categories that a reader brings to a reading, and the categories in which that reading itself is placed—the learned social and political categories, and the physical categories into which a library is divided—constantly modify one another in ways that appear, over the years, more or less arbitrary or more or less imaginative. . . . Whatever categories have been chosen, every library tyrannizes the act of reading and forces the reader—the curious reader, the alert reader—to rescue the book from the category to which it has been condemned.[9]

This subversive rescue mission, I must add, is one the library promotes in its own subversive way. If the library truly wanted order it would have one ultimate book on each topic. There it is—your answer. But that is precisely what libraries don't do. Instead, they celebrate the multiplicities of meaning by seeking out dissension and putting it together.

Umberto Eco, in an address on the opening of a new library, portrayed a nightmarish institution in which rules make no sense: "The Information Desk for readers must be inaccessible." "Borrowing shall be discouraged." "Ideally, no readers should be allowed inside the library." The rules in this library exist for the purposes of exclusion, rulemaking taken to a ridiculous extreme. Fortunately he is able to describe libraries he has visited where the rules don't exclude readers—or the opportunity for them to make unexpected discoveries:

> I enter to work, in true English empirical fashion; instead I find myself among the commentators on Aristotle, I wind up on the wrong floor, I go into a section, say Medicine, in which I never thought to stray and suddenly I stumble on the works about Galen, full of philosophical references. This way, a library is an adventure.[10]

It is an adventure that can happen in spite of—and because of—the ways in which knowledge is categorized and mapped.

Why is it that the library as a place where knowledge is ordered and regulated can also offer means of transcending that order? I think it all has to do with the experience of libraries. Unlike the boundless and endlessly mutable virtual library, a physical library is a crossroads of place and space.

The humanistic geographer Yi-Fu Tuan described the importance of experience in constructing reality. Through experience, we reach out beyond ourselves and know what is beyond us. It employs our senses in the categorization of things. Further, we use our experience of place to create a sense of how things might be in places we've never been. Being oriented to a place gives us confidence because we are rooted in personal, sensory experience. It is ours in a way that imparted knowledge isn't until we have been able to relate it to our life experience in some fundamental way. As Tuan points out, "Learning is rarely at the level of explicit and formal knowledge."[11] That would seem to fly in the face of what colleges are all about—yet librarians know, perhaps better than anyone, that the experience a student gains in wrestling with ideas through research is far more than the sum of the information gathered in the process. In the end, what they know pales in comparison to what they have learned about knowing. Research is, after all, experiential education.

"Place is security, space is freedom," Tuan says. "We are attached to the one and long for the other."[12] To conceptualize space—that is, to understand what we don't yet know—we must first locate ourselves in relation to the world by being rooted in a place that we know through experience. Knowing our place gives us a reference point for experiencing space. The library, as a physical place, is small enough that it can be experienced and mapped. In fact, libraries aid in that mapping by sorting out knowledge in a grid that can be perceived as having meaning, if not all meanings. The coordinates established through the experience of a library, then, can orient the explorer heading out into the unknown. Without familiarity and a sense of belonging in a centered and known (if necessarily limited) world of knowledge, the vast space of the Library of Babel cannot be explored because we feel inevitably disoriented and lost.

The first visit to a research library is a trip to the unknown, and its unfamiliarity is intimidating for students. It takes time to develop enough experience that space turns into place. I recently spent several sabbatical months in Manhattan. On my first foray into the Humanities and Social Sciences Research Library on Fifth Avenue, I climbed the steps where lions guard the door, went into the great marble and gilt entrance hall, wandered aimlessly for a few minutes, making far too much noise on the polished floor with my Doc Martens, and fled without even having located the reading room. The glory of the public library as a nineteenth-century temple of knowledge and civic identity has been lovingly restored in recent years, but that glory made me feel like bag lady trying to catch a nap in the lobby of the Ritz. It would only be a matter of time before someone noticed and threw me out.

I went back later to brave the lions and within a few visits felt at home, filling out call slips and waiting for my numbers to come up on the board as if I'd done it all my life. Before my first visit, I knew that everyone is welcome there—you don't even have to have a reader's card or be a resident of the city—but knowing it and experiencing it were two very different things. I needed to develop the sense of place gained only through repeated visits.

The academic library is no doubt at least as intimidating to students at first encounter as the library on Fifth Avenue was to me. But it waits patiently for them to come back, explore further, and eventually claim a piece of it as their own, as I did with that battered wooden table beside a window in my remembered library. They gain a sense of place—and with it, of security—and can then venture on beyond it into space—gaining the freedom of knowing that not all is within these walls; not all is known, much has yet to be discovered. In a similar sense, the permanence of texts in real space offer the novice researcher a chance to return again and again, not just to check and see if a text is still there (as often virtual texts are not) but to understand it better. The text does not change, but the reading does. As Doug Brent has put it, "Evoking meaning from texts is a recursive, not a linear process." The permanence of a physical text available in a library enables rereading; each time a text is queried with new knowledge, it will "evoke a new virtual work from it."[13]

Sven Birkerts uses a cartographic metaphor when he argues that print culture offers closure, where screen culture represents open-endedness. Ironically the "closure" implied in a book opens as it is arrayed beside other works, connecting them in ways that that the electronic text—hyperlinks and all—cannot achieve. "A piece of data, of information, only becomes a piece of knowledge when it can be understood as the answer to a question," Birkerts argues:

> We cannot find answers if we cannot formulate questions. We cannot formulate questions if we cannot grasp context. . . . The physicalized text, its location in space, subject to ordering systems, manifested this—multiplicity offset by specificity, the enormous terrain contained as by a map.[14]

In contrast, the screen offers no peripheral view: "Reading from a screen is like traveling from coast to coast with only adjoining local maps as guides."[15] Because everything in cyberspace is potentially adjacent to everything else—we are all here, there is no there there—it exists with no context, no depth of field, no perspective. We cannot map such a space, nor find ourselves in it.

My virtual library has given me a sense of my place in the world of knowledge. It isn't even there anymore, not in a physical sense, but it is mine through experience. With that grounding in experience, I have a map of knowledge, with coordinates from which I can triangulate my way into the remote unknown. I worry about students who arrive at college knowing how to use an Internet browser, but not how to use a library, often avoiding staking a claim in the library because it isn't familiar, because they haven't yet experienced it. That false sense of security they have from the familiar—of knowing where to click, how to print—disguises the fact that on the Web, they aren't sure where they are, or where texts come from, or which can be trusted.

My sense of the world of knowledge can be unrolled like a big map. I can spread it out wider than any computer screen, find the marker that says "you are here," and chart my course across wide distances, aware of scale, recognizing landmarks. The academic library should be a place that students lay claim to as a base camp, cartographers beginning an adventure into the unknown. We need to help them brave the lions (who are, after all, just big, friendly cats named Patience and Fortitude) and come inside again and again until they have found a table and a window and made it theirs.

Notes

1. Roland Barthes, "The Death of the Author," in *Image—Music—Text*, trans. Stephen Hearn (New York: Hill and Wang, 1977), 142–48. It's interesting that the influence of Barthes's challenge to the hegemony of the individual author has gained popularity just as copyright law has been revised in favor of intellectual property owners, suggesting reports of the author's death are greatly exaggerated.

2. Gertrude Himmelfarb, "Revolution in the Library," *American Scholar* 66(2) 1997: 197–204.

3. Thomas Mann, "The Importance of Books, Free Access, and Libraries As Place—and the Dangerous Inadequacy of the Information Science Paradigm," *Journal of Academic Librarianship* 27(4) 2001: 276.

4. Jorge Luis Borges, "The Library of Babel," in *Collected Fictions*, trans. Andrew Hurley (New York: Viking, 1998), 112–18.

5. Borges, "Library of Babel," 115–16.

6. Borges, "Library of Babel," 116.

7. Christopher R. Martin and Bettina Fabos, "Wiring the Kids: The TV Ad Blitz to Get the Internet into Home and School," *Images: A Journal of Film and Popular Culture* 7 (1998), February 14, 2002, at www.imagesjournal.com/issue07/features/wiringthekids.htm.

8. Alberto Manguel, *A History of Reading* (New York: Viking, 1996), 198.

9. Manguel, *History of Reading*, 198–99.

10. Umberto Eco, "De Bibliotheca," trans. N. F.–G. *Bostonia* 1 (Spring 1993), 57–60, reprinted in an e-mail message posted to Collib-L discussion list by Larry Oberg (August 21, 1997).

11. Yi-Fu Tuan, *Place and Space: The Perspective of Experience* (Minneapolis: University of Minnesota Press, 1977), 199.

12. Tuan, *Place and Space*, 3.

13. Doug Brent, *Reading As Rhetorical Invention: Knowledge, Persuasion, and the Teaching of Research-Based Writing* (Urbana, Ill.: NCTE, 1992), 109.

14. Sven Birkerts, "Sense and Semblance: The Implications of Virtuality," in *Readings* (St. Paul, Minn.: Graywolf, 1999), 51–52.

15. Birkerts, "Sense and Semblence," 43.

Yo, que me figuraba el Paraiso Bajo la especie de una biblioteca.

I, who have always thought of Paradise in form and image as a library.

—Jorge Luis Borges

CHAPTER SIX

Ketchup Has Always Been a Vegetable

Margaret Law and Randy Reichardt

> You got to be very careful if you don't know where you're going, because you might not get there.
>
> —Yogi Berra

At conferences, on listservs, in journals, and in our own discussions over coffee, we lament the way that students are today. We perceive that they are not the same as they used to be: they lack focus, can't read as well as they once could, and are not good critical thinkers. We worry that they are overly dependent on electronic resources, that they are always multitasking. We fret that their criteria for selecting information resources are not the ones that we value. Instead of valid, authoritative, and comprehensive, they often choose easy, fast, and available. We are anxious about whether anyone teaches them to think for themselves anymore. In short, we are in danger of turning into their parents.

Beloit College publishes its "Mindset List" at the beginning of every academic year. The list is "a compilation of items that indicate the viewpoint and frame of reference of entering students"[1] (i.e., undergrads beginning their first year of postsecondary education immediately after high school). This is an effort to remind faculty that every new cohort of students brings with it the framework of the environment in which each student was raised. As the world changes, so does this framework of experience. We tend to use images and words that are comfortable and meaningful to ourselves in our interactions with students. The annual Beloit list reminds us that those same images and words may not resonate with today's students.

Who are we? We are the ones who remember when ketchup wasn't a vegetable. Unlike those whom we teach, we were raised to know ketchup as a condiment, to be added to hamburgers, hot dogs, and even Kraft Dinner! We are librarians who are well educated, with multiple degrees, and because of where we work and teach, we are products of academia. Our work is complex, and we put a lot of love and energy into it. What we do is important to us, and we believe strongly that is has value and worth.

We typically care about our users and want their experiences in our libraries to be positive and rewarding. Money is not our major motivator, or we would have considered law or investment banking rather than librarianship. Instead, "another satisfied customer" is more likely to be our mantra. In our public-service capacity, contact with our users is important. As we work with them, either in classes or one-on-one, they learn who we are and what we do, and the library gets a human face. It becomes more than a repository for books and computers or the place where reserve material will be found. Ultimately, we want students to be our "partners in learning," rather than leaving them to do it alone. At the same time, we work toward supporting student development of new research skills and abilities, which they will carry with them throughout their academic and professional lives.

We want students to develop the skills that form the foundation of information literacy. In the librarian's perfect world, students learn to recognize when they need information and why they need it. They understand the differences among assignments, background reading, and problem solving. They learn to find and use information sources such as databases and resource guides to lead them to the information they require. As librarians, we obsess all too often that these sources must be the best available and the most comprehensive. (Why is this so important to us? Will students be short-changed if they don't find every article, conference paper, patent, standard, or website relevant to their research question? The answer is probably no.)

Once students have identified the best resources, we want them to locate and acquire them, read and digest the information within, and incorporate that information into their existing knowledge base for use in their work. In the end, our ultimate goal is behavior modification. From not knowing what to do or where to begin, students may learn a better way to do research through our guidance and direction.

Who are "they"? Generally, the objects of our concern are first- and second-year undergraduate students, who live in a whirlwind at university or college. Many are away from home for the first time, experimenting with who they are and how they will live in the world. This is the time for sex, drugs, and rock 'n' roll. As far as generalizations are true, they want things that are fast and easy to use. They have many things to do and see, and many of them want to move along quickly. Because of other demands on their time, both social and economic, they tend not to function in a traditional forty-hour week. For them, "good" information is stuff that is available twenty-four hours each day; they live in a 24/7 environment.

First- and second-year students' primary motivation is generally to meet the requirements of their instructors. They are truly consumers of just-enough, just-in-time delivery. They need to get good marks, and as the economic climate changes, they become increasingly competitive. This places a higher value on academic marks than on intellectual enquiry. In a simplistic sense, activities that don't generate high marks are of less value. In their perfect world, instruction would occur one-on-one, helping them solve problems as they occurred rather than teaching them a range of skills that they may or may not need later.

Younger students often see themselves as customers of the educational process rather than participants. They want the service for which they have paid, delivered when and where they want it. They may not appreciate our efforts to mold them into better students, as they may not see this as part of the psychological contract between customer and service provider.

Are they really any different than we were at that age? Professors and librarians used to bemoan the fact that students were browsing the periodical collection, looking for articles rather than using the periodical index. Anything that seemed close enough to the topic worked, without resorting to using the catalog and without exercising any particular critical-thinking skills. Who among us hasn't chosen an essay topic for the ease of finding information rather than personal interest or the opportunity to learn? Is this any different from choosing the first three resources that pop up on the screen in front of them?

So what are the implications, if any? As librarians, with a commitment to provide service and add value to the academic enterprise, we may do well to begin our work with observation without judgment. Students are not like us, but we need to remember that we were also not like us when we were young undergraduates. In their first and second year, students often do not have a good context for evaluating resources. In fact, they don't have enough life experience to have good context for evaluating much of life. We need to allow them to learn through their own mistakes, including the selection of poor resources and weak arguments. Experiencing the consequences of such actions is a valuable learning experience for them. If they don't know where they are going and don't get there, are they the worse for wear? Have they lost anything?

Our true value to students and researchers is to discover their needs and wants and then to find innovative ways to meet these rather than being critical of them. Most undergraduates have grown up in a very different environment than most librarians—with more technology, more media, and more choices, and with everything moving at a faster pace. We need to support them with the skills they need to succeed in this environment, not wish for a kinder, gentler, more intellectual time. If we insist on our own way, we will lose the opportunities to influence them and to help them develop some of the skills and values that are dear to us.

How does this affect our view of service delivery, in particular bibliographic instruction by this name or any other? How do we maintain standards of critical thinking, assessment, and ethical use of information, while meeting students where they are? First, we need to apply our own critical-thinking skills to the issue. What is it that students really need, and can we test for the impact of our own assumptions about what we think they need or should need? To what extent do we allow outside factors to influence our work in this area, including the constraints of time, money, and tradition? We must beware of falling into a competency trap; all of us like to do things at which we are good, and we like to teach because we have developed a high level of skill and comfort doing it. How, then, do we question objectively whether or not the instruction we give is still relevant?

A recurring theme in discussion groups and listservs is the lack of research into measurable changes in students and their perceptions. Questions touch on the possibilities of neurological change that result from exposure to different media and reductions in attention span.

Can our perception that students born into the post-MTV generation are really different be supported by hard research? The post-MTV generation has been exposed to visual media in which images change every second. Has this actually affected their ability to concentrate? Does it make them impatient when they are doing research? The library community is not likely to conduct this research; we need to seek out and use research from other fields.

Arguably, our job as librarians is to collect information, arrange it, and provide good access to it. If we were to do the best (but impossible) job of that, we would design the perfect search engine, one that always provides resources in order of quality. Then we could meet our requirement that students would use excellent resources and still meet their needs for speed and ease of use. Much of our teaching and reference work is a result of needing to fill the gap between the needs of users and the quixotic ways in which we have chosen to arrange information and provide access to it.

Arguably again, our job is not to conduct psychological or neurological research. It may, however, be our province to conduct research into the information-seeking behavior of our users. This seems like an added burden to our already heavy workload, but it may be an essential one. Continuing to focus on doing what we do now, always trying to improve how we do it, probably doesn't serve us well in the long term. The issue may be that we have to set aside some of the things we do now in order to make time to think about where to go next.

How do we instruct students whom we may never see? How do we put a human face on the library if students only interact with us electronically? How do we assess the success of information seeking behavior of people we don't know? The beginning of change needs to come from our values and beliefs about what we do. If we are not willing to abandon some of our current beliefs and workload in order to tackle questions like this, we run the risk of becoming entirely irrelevant and existing only as legends in our own minds.

We are not the only ones who need to make some of these changes in values and direction. It is an old adage that "what gets counted gets done." As long as library directors compete with each other in the statistical wars and academic administrations use statistical comparisons for allocating resources, it is difficult, if not impossible, to abandon our current mode of teaching. When tabulating classes taught and number of attendees, the impetus is to keep these numbers increasing continually. This does not even recognize our current situation—that much teaching now occurs online or in nonclassroom settings. That certainly does not give us room to maneuver and to move away from tried-and-true statistics generators toward growth that may be immeasurable. It is hard to win accolades by proving that something that has always been part of the library's contribution to the academic community may not longer be relevant.

Undergraduate students are not like us, nor should they be. We have much to offer them, but they also have much to offer us. We have traditional skills that have served us well and have some validity in the new world. Students have skills in filtering input from many sources simultaneously, dealing with many formats and evaluating in different ways. It is important for us to be clear about our professional responsibility as librarians, including understanding and respecting the boundaries between our roles and those of faculty and students. It is through this clarity that we will be able to focus our efforts in the most appropriate way.

If one of our desired outcomes is that students are motivated to find and use excellent resources, it is critical that there be negative consequences to finding and using poor resources. Given the motivating power of grades, it is only the teaching faculty members who are able to provide this negative consequence. Where, then, does our role overlap with theirs? Perhaps the real method for motivating students to become information literate is to spend more time with faculty, making sure that students are not rewarded for poor information choices.

In order to overcome the limitations that we all work with, in particular time and money, we must focus our energies on the issues that fall within our professional responsibility and will make the most difference. We need to be sure of where we are going, so that we know when we get there.

Note

1. See www.beloit.edu/~pubaff/mindset.

I find television very educational. The minute somebody turns it on, I go to the library and read a good book.

—Groucho Marx

CHAPTER SEVEN

Creating That Teachable Moment

Ilene F. Rockman

The mind is like a parachute; it works best when it is open.

—Anonymous

We have all seen those glassy-eyed undergraduate students with wandering minds who seem to be trapped in some far-off land during our course-integrated sessions or information-literacy workshops.

For some unknown reason, they are not tuned in to their environment. Their minds are not open, and the educational conditions are not right for us to make our teaching points or for them to engage in the learning opportunities at hand. These students are not interested in what is occurring in the class, and they are not as actively engaged in the content of the lesson as we would like them to be. Even when we deliberately incorporate active learning opportunities, they hold back, and it is a challenge to reach them.

The harsh reality is that these (and any other) students learn best when they are motivated and, most importantly, when their minds are open to learning.

How can we, as instruction librarians, create that teachable moment when the conditions and timing are right for learning to occur? How can we take into account our students' intellectual abilities and their innate curiosities and develop educational environments in which students are excited and enthusiastic about learning? How can we appropriately engage students in their own learning processes—reaching them where they are—in the here and now?

One strategy is to turn to the late Madeleine Hunter for guidance and inspiration. Dr. Hunter, a former educational psychologist, teacher, and principal of the UCLA University Elementary School, was a small, yet magnetic, woman whose ideas about pedagogy and learning have had a large influence on a variety of scholars and practitioners over the past few decades. Her ideas have held up well over time and are easily transferable to today's information-literacy setting.

Dr. Hunter was an advocate of causal relationships to promote student learning. In her book *Mastery Teaching*,[1] she elaborates on a model that includes components such as the following components:.

1. *Anticipatory Set:* This is the "hook" to get the students ready to learn and involved in the content of the lesson, whether it is how to search precisely and evaluate information quality or how to apply the research process to a "real-life" information need. Dr. Hunter challenges us to think about what we, as teachers, will do to reach students at their current levels and then take them to the level where we want them to be. This step is a preparation to assess student readiness to learn and to influence sustained learning—with some fun and unpredictability along the way.

   A successful technique to employ is to start the class session with a provocative question that will wake the students up, pique their curiosity, and begin their creative-thinking processes. It is fine to learn by "doing," but it is also desirable to learn by "thinking." Some educators even suggest that if you talk fast, students will think fast. Whatever style is comfortable for you is the right one to use; however, recognize that, although it may seem serendipitous, you can intentionally create a "teachable moment" by using the strategy of beginning with an unexpected question.

For example, to immediately gain the cognitive attention of the class you could ask one of the following questions:

- "How is managing information like conducting a symphony orchestra?"
- "How is searching for information like grocery shopping?"
- "How is evaluating information like buying a new pair of shoes?"

A seemingly meaningless pairing of unrelated events generates a moment that instantaneously grasps the attention of students by piquing their curiosities and asking them neutral questions they have never heard before and that have no right or wrong answers.

Moreover, since first impressions are so important, these challenging questions, presented at the beginning of the instructional session, have a greater likelihood of being remembered. They also creatively challenge even the most uninterested students to focus their attention. By zeroing in on the content to be learned, hooking the students into their past experiences and prior knowledge, and then triggering their visual memories, learning can actually be accelerated.

Now that you have successfully reached the students, the next step is to move them along in the learning process using their own interest, curiosity, and motivation as collaborative partners.

2. *Input:* This critical step requires us to clearly explain the instructional purpose of the lesson to the students. Why is it important for them to listen and pay attention?

From salient discussions that result from answering the "anticipatory set" questions, the instructor-librarian can easily segue into explaining the objective of the instructional session, clearing up any past confusion, and helping the students to understand how they can be successful in completing their assignments.

Dr. Hunter reminds us that students will usually expend more effort and, thus, increase their learning, if they know what is realistically expected of them and why is it important. Because students frequently do not (or cannot) make these connections for themselves, it is important for the librarian to do so. For example, mentioning that "today we are going to explore various websites to discern fact from fiction so that you will be able to critically evaluate the information you receive from the Internet, and make more informed decisions" helps us to clarify learner expectations and set the foundation, rationale, and context for learning.

Being creative, adaptive, and innovative, and having a sense of humor during this process also helps, as does an awareness that one's state of mind (open or closed) relates to one's ability to teach or learn effectively. Common sense and direct observation also tell us that a relationship exists between openness to learning and resultant learner performance. As teachers, our challenge is to find and take advantage of those open windows to create "teachable moments" and to be flexible, comfortable, and confident enough to allow for whatever serendipitous learning opportunities may occur along the way.

3. *Modeling:* How will we confidently lead by example so students will assign significance to what we do and, thus, follow (e.g., learn more effectively and efficiently for themselves)?

If we are teaching how to find information on a topic by searching through and using a variety of information sources, we can exemplify stellar searching characteristics. We can show and explain preferred techniques, stopping along the way to inform the students about what we are doing and why it is important. We can also use these instructional moments to elaborate on and underscore the points we want to communicate clearly to students. By doing so, they will clearly remember what they have seen, sharpen their memories, and incorporate appropriate searching techniques into their own styles of behavior.

For example, if we want students to understand clearly the intricacies of Boolean searching, we can create a concrete visual image of a Venn diagram on a blackboard or whiteboard to show the differences between searching with the operators and, or, and not. We can then apply this technique to searching for information about the Middle East in various full-text databases, using both keyword and controlled-vocabulary terms, comparing the different content of the articles retrieved based upon the use of the different operators. These results might lend themselves into a discussion of effective methods for expressing a concept and selecting search terms, different writing styles and content included in popular or scholarly articles, methods to adjust search strategies to increase precision in searching, what type of information may not included in certain databases (e.g., newspaper articles or government publications), and how to interpret and evaluate search results.

Such models can be both visual and verbal—the key is knowing when and how to use them in order to accelerate the learning process for the students.

4. *Checking for Understanding*: This next step is key to the teaching-learning process. It suggests that we ask ourselves the following questions:

- "Now that the lesson has concluded, what strategies will we use to make sure that student learning has occurred?"
- "What will we do to effectively diagnose the extent of student learning and offer remediation, if necessary?"

An ineffective approach is to ask at the conclusion of the instructional session, "Are there any questions?" or to say, "You all understand, don't you?"

A more effective approach is to provide a way for the students to directly apply what they have heard and seen to a completely new problem-based situation that will challenge them to immediately demonstrate the extent of their knowledge.

Reinforcing the concepts of the lesson with assignments that will ask the students to stretch beyond their current levels of awareness and to strive to become confident, independent thinkers is the preferred method. For example, if students are asked to find a website that is biased, they will first have to understand the concepts of fact versus opinion before they can intelligently identify such sites. They will then need to apply appropriate evaluation criteria to the selected sites to show or prove that bias is part and parcel of the site.

5. *Guided Practice:* Although practice doesn't make perfect, giving students a controlled environment in which to apply directly the points they have heard and seen is a step in the right direction. The direct application of knowledge through independent problem-solving opportunities under the watchful supervision of a teacher or more capable peer is one of the best ways to internalize and remember learning and ultimately to transfer it to a new situation.

Giving students sufficient time to acquire confidence in applying their skills to a different setting (moving from the familiar to the unknown) is critical for their understanding and for learning to occur.

Whenever possible in our library-instructional sessions, we need to ask ourselves if we have allocated enough time for students to engage in "hands-on" practice, either individually or in collaborative teams or work groups. This practice can revolve around activities such as comparing the results of keyword versus controlled-vocabulary searching in an online catalog, evaluating the content of two full-text articles from two different sources written during two different time periods or contrasting the accounts of an historical event from the perspectives of a primary and a secondary source.

Providing immediate feedback, reassurance, and encouragement while the students grasp the new concepts of searching for and evaluating information will insure and sustain their interest in continuing to learn and grow into critical consumers of information. By allowing sufficient time for students to practice and being willing to "coach" them to refine their search techniques, we can promote understanding, insight, and ultimately, learning.

Application to Information Literacy

Creating that "teachable moment" can be both planned and unplanned. Conditions are best for learning when the instructor either has the confidence, strength, and ability to create a challenging and creative environment for individual discovery and inquiry or is flexible and nimble enough to take advantage of whatever opportunity comes along to promote serendipitous learning.

Certainly, being able to help students understand how to identify, organize, use, and evaluate information to answer a given problem in the context of a well-written class assignment (integrated into the learning outcomes of an academic discipline) is an ideal goal. Under these conditions, using problem-based learning principles, student learning lends itself most to being retained. In addition, when the sassignment is clearly explained, when instructor modeling and encouragement occur, and when unhurried guided practice is available, favorable conditions for student learning are increased.

When students are asked to draw on their own past experiences and prior knowledge, using their creative abilities to find, evaluate, and use information from a variety of sources, and when they have success in doing so, they are well on their way to becoming information-literate. Confident in their analytical skills and reasoning abilities, and stimulated by their own intrinsic motivation, they are better able to solve any future information need whenever it arises.

Most importantly, they know how to learn, they enjoy the challenge of learning, and they are not dismayed or flustered by a constantly changing information environment. As a result, they have gained the requisite knowledge to be continual learners throughout their lifetimes, having been skillfully nurtured and guided along by that "teachable moment."

Note

1. Madeline Hunter, *Mastery Teaching* (El Segundo, Calif.: TIP Publications, 1982). See also Darlene L. Stewart, *Creating the Teachable Moment* (Blue Ridge Summit, Pa.: Tab Books, 1993).

The mediocre teacher tells.
The good teacher explains.
The superior teacher demonstrates.
The great teacher inspires.

—William Arthur Ward

CHAPTER EIGHT

A Bookless Society—Who Says?

Diana D. Shonrock

The bookless society is the hallucination of the online addicts,
network neophytes and library automation insiders.

—Clifford Stoll

I know we're heading for a bookless society.

—Will Manley

We hear many arguments about the potential for a bookless society. But
the dispute often distracts us from the real issue: a bookless society is
not so much about paper and ink as it is about thinking and a state of
mind. What do we want students to achieve during their college years?
What obstacles lie in their way, and how can we help students overcome them? Are computers contributing to the solutions or are they
part of the problem?

65

A crucial part of the answer to such questions involves knowing how children learn. Specifically, do they learn better in social groups or alone online? For me the answer is simple: learning demands proficiency in reading and writing, and well-developed social skills. If we wish to destroy learning, to create a world of isolates who don't know how to get along with each other and have no reason to do so, I can think of no better way than to shove children into cyberspace and tell them to learn and communicate electronically. Yet this seems to be the direction we are heading with our "bookless society."

Clifford Stoll voiced these concerns by asking whether computers teach reading and a love of books and whether they teach social skills. He answered by pointing out that Web pages are practically all graphics, so rather than encouraging reading and creative writing, they actually promote a copy-and-paste attitude. And while "tomorrow's jobs, like today's, will belong to those with social skills," time spent behind a keyboard dulls these essential abilities.[1]

What are our goals as academic librarians? For me they are to promote learning, to encourage critical thinking, and to assist students in doing quality research. In looking for a framework to help me organize my thoughts and structure my responses to these challenges, I agree with Bruce Harley, Megan Dreger and Patricia Knobloch.[2] that three key issues facing academic libraries are "consumerism, superficiality and knowledge fragmentation." I would add one other—technology—since it affects more than ever how we live and learn.

Consumerism

As consumers in a fast-paced society, students are accustomed to obtaining what they want when they want it. They expect to find whatever information they are looking for quickly and easily, and they convince themselves that they can fulfill all their research needs by using the Web alone. In the process, they devalue the research process. They tend to embrace the ATM approach to consumer satisfaction, believing that assistance and guidance from others (at least librarians) may actually hinder the research process.

On the other hand, they are comfortable networking with each other, using electronic means such as instant messaging, cell phones, and e-mail. Perhaps we should take a page from their book and inter-act in such modes. The variety could help keep their attention and would render us in their minds as being more up-to-date.

Superficiality

Students want to find only the information required for their assign-ments and no more. As electronic images become increasingly om-nipresent, their study habits seem to suffer. Shorter attention spans, inadequate preparation, placing emphasis on grades rather than on learning, and an interest in the surface and not the substance of things are among the newer ways of thinking linked to students. According to several researchers, this emphasis on quick results will only accelerate. Students will become even more likely to be satisfied with bits and pieces of information and will devote even less time to aggregating these into knowledge.

Perhaps the greatest challenge facing librarians will be to provide the context in which students can learn to think critically about their course assignments and understand how these might apply to their daily lives.

Knowledge Fragmentation

The Web is perhaps the ultimate example of knowledge fragmentation. It has been aptly described as "a huge vandalized library":

> Someone has destroyed the catalog and removed the front matter, in-dexes, etc. from hundreds of thousands of books and torn and scattered what remains. . . . "Surfing" is the process of sifting through this disorgan-ized mess in the hope of coming across some useful fragments of text and images that can be related to other fragments. The Net is even worse than a vandalized library because thousands of additional unorganized frag-ments are added daily by the myriad cranks, sages, and persons with time on their hands who launch their unfiltered messages into cyberspace.[3]

The Web allows users to jump from page to page, extracting infor-mation from numerous locations with no concern for the relevance of these ideas to each other or to the whole. Fragmentation overempha-sizes subjectivity and impedes critical thinking. A student may retrieve a page with relevant information, but the provenance and purpose of the page remain unknown.

This decline in critical thinking is fostered by the fact that some of the online services are marketed directly to students. For example, it is a simple task to lift a passage from a large work, such as Uncle Tom's Cabin, and insert it into a paper without the student understanding its context or its relation to Harriet Beecher Stowe's thought or intent. Certainly students have taken information out of context before, but at least the whole item was offered. And so were its neighbors on the shelf, and not just the few items for which a vendor had acquired copyright permission. Herein lies the importance of critical thinking and academic honesty.

Technology

Technology makes life more convenient and enjoyable, but it also affects work, family, and the economy in unpredictable ways. It introduces new forms of tension and distraction and poses new threats to the cohesion of our physical communities.

Technorealism is a movement that questions the value of developments in communication and computing, and some of these apply to us as librarians. Technologies are not neutral, information is not knowledge, and wiring our schools will not save them nor encourage learning. Statistics are beginning to show that students do not learn best in front of a computer screen. The computer is only a tool. It is like many others we can use to promote learning, but it is not the whole answer. Technorealism demands that we think about the role that tools play in human evolution and everyday life. Integral to this perspective is our understanding that the current tide of technological transformation, while important and powerful, is actually a continuation of waves of change that have taken place throughout history.

Technology is also expensive. How do we educate our patrons about the costs and benefits of electronic resources, about the difference between the "free" Internet with its often less-than-reliable resources, and the quality of the subscription databases available in our libraries?

At the same time, what happens when a university replaces a print encyclopedia that it has purchased new every fifth year for $1,500, with its online version, at annual subscription cost of $10,000 to $12,000 per year? While doing so does offer broader access and possibly greater use, what about the loss of touch and feel? How does the substitution of electronic for print access change the dynamics of the junior-high-school history-project groups that socialize at the public or school library around a table covered with volumes of *World Book Encyclopedia*? Are there real problems when students aren't touching print books and journals and taking them off the shelf, since some of the skills acquired are indeed social?

Students' use of the Internet is also troubling because it is "free," increasing the temptation to cut and paste without attribution, and also because it is so large. Many students fall into a double pit believing that "everything is on the Web," and if it isn't, it doesn't exist.

And this erroneous idea is not restricted to students. Though less than 10 percent of academic journals are currently online, some instructors and college officials believe that students can get virtually anything they need online (or at least enough that they can do a decent job of research). Digitizing monographic collections is a costly and monumental task that nonlibrarians often don't understand. We must do a better job in teaching them the challenges of technology and costs.

Strategies for Change

As universities have grown without the funding and faculty to match, students have begun to recognize a need for community. While the brick-and-mortar library may not grow, this is not necessarily bad. The library will become more virtual, but librarians will still be the collection monitors and evaluators.

A variety of authors have pondered ways to attract more students to libraries and engage them once they are inside. Among their suggestions, several of which have been tested in real library settings, are these:

- Author readings and/or signing
- In-house cafes or coffee shop
- Plush sofas and chairs
- Comfortable browsing or leisure reading collections
- Counseling and advising services
- Exhibit areas

- Campus stores
- Media commons

Even though some of these ideas may only superficially get to the heart of the matter, they do encourage social interaction. Such simple things as welcoming service points and well-equipped group-study areas, along with provisions for laptop computers, wireless technology, and one-stop-shopping for computer workstations, will do as much to provide us with access to students. We must constantly ask ourselves which of the things we are already doing pays the greatest dividends, which things already bring students close to us?

And we must capitalize on every opportunity to interact with students once they are inside our libraries. We must make time for them, talk with them about their research, listen well, and do all that we can to encourage the flow of information in both directions. We must avoid situations where we might come across as "dictators" and, instead, become companions in the information quest.

Strategies to Deliver Resources and Services to Students

We should focus on delivering our services and collections in a way that is already comfortable and familiar to students—via technology. We should first acknowledge the library website for what it really is— a means of delivery for remote resources and services. Then we must exploit all possible means of advertising those resources and services. In addition to e-mail and fax, we must consider using the interactive technology for reference and delivering more than resources and services to students outside the library.

We must be more involved in campus activities, such as student orientation; campus instruction and mentoring; tutoring programs; academic, social, and cultural events; and community service projects. Perhaps we should even consider holding court outside the library. What roles could we play if the library became the venue for access to other student services, such as tutoring and other academic-success programs? Budget constraints across our campuses can be the opportunity we need to become a "full-service" provider, to link the academic community to our resources more directly. People have long seen public libraries as places of community, but academic libraries have long shunned that role. This does not mean that we must provide those services ourselves but rather that we must become more open and welcoming and less isolationist in sharing our facilities with these outside services. Why is it that every other room on the campus can be assigned, but we often covet our space and close our doors?

Strategies to Make Reference and Instruction More Facilitative

Our instruction must provide more general principles and less information; that is, we should concentrate on helping students learn a relevant, coherent progression of skills that leads toward self-reliance. We must teach students to critically evaluate sources of information and to be more concerned with finding the meaning and value of an information package than finding an answer.

We must reevaluate traditional services and focus on the significant variables that affect action. The principles of information literacy that we have worked so hard to develop must be shared outside our walls and followed more stringently within. Academic librarians unwittingly contribute to information's unwarranted status whenever we devote more attention to how students find information than to how they evaluate and use what they find. We should not be in the business of teaching students how to use the library. Rather, we should be in the business of teaching students how to think through their research problems and how to perform a variety of intellectual tasks. We must teach critical-thinking skills, not classification systems.

Our expertise, aside from the ability to use an increasingly wide variety of information resources, lies in our ability to integrate critical teaching into the learning processes. The highest value we can add to our existing services, activities, and programs is our knowledge. We must also remember that most people use and seek information in a social context. Values such as trust, responsibility, and critical thinking can only be imparted person-to-person. While face-to-face exchanges are best, live chat reference experiences offer a suitable surrogate and are attractive and valuable to our remote online users.

It is by interacting with students in a one-on-one environment that academic librarians will have a positive effect on the quality of the students' learning environment.

The difference between training and facilitation is that the latter requires changes in attitudes and behavior. As we take the time to learn more about ourselves as teachers and about ways to interact more effectively with students, we will learn to direct—not dictate—thought. Students who have learned to think for themselves are suspicious of the motives of any instructor who tells them how to think instead of offering room for exploration of ideas.

A student came to me recently and asked if I thought that Shel Silverstein's book The Giving Tree was extremely sexist and racist. She explained that another teacher had told her this was true. She wanted to know if I believed it. What I tried to show her, and what I would want other students to understand, is that it is most important what the book says to her, what she believes, and with whom she is going to share the book. The issue was for her to examine what she heard and make an educated decision—not just believe what an instructor had said.

The Learning Community Movement and the Human Element of Libraries

At many universities over the past ten years, groups generally described as "learning communities" have been organized. They have been created in response to a number of concerns, including the increasing numbers of students, shrinking faculty size, sense of isolation often experienced by new students, and a growing dependence on technology to teach.

Because learning communities allow students to learn in a more interdisciplinary manner, it is important to consider ways of making them intellectually stimulating and challenging. One often underutilized enhancement is creative linking between the e-library and students to emphasize information literacy and the interactive nature of information. So while on one hand we drive our students to more and more "solitary" computer use and larger classes, we can counteract the negative aspects of such experiences and create community through the formation of smaller groups with like interests.

Here at Iowa State University, as a result of the Learning Community movement, we have realized an increase in retention rate over four years of around 12 percent for students who take part in learning communities.

Librarians can enhance the role of learning communities on an academic campus. They can expand diversity through their introduction of information-literacy and critical-thinking skills and address factors such as the following:

- Students' ability to define, refine, and articulate information needs
- Costs and benefits of acquiring information
- Identification of methods of acquiring information
- Determination of how to use information effectively
- Understanding of the ethical, legal, and social issues surrounding the use of information.

We can also provide a forum for the introduction and discussion of such ideas as intellectual freedom and the issues related to censorship and filtering. We can aid in the development of skills that open students to new ideas. Libraries have been slow to become involved, but it is encouraging to note the proliferation of workshops and conference sessions focused on such programs.

Conclusion

As instructors and librarians, we must maintain the lines of communication with students and encourage lifelong learning through the teaching of critical-thinking skills. Libraries should not be about tools and databases but about ways to discover and ways to transform information into knowledge. The "bookless society" really does have more to do with a state of mind than with the state of print versus electronic information. What we want to preserve is the intellectual curiosity and human interaction that libraries and librarians provide.

Notes

1. Clifford Stoll, "Who Needs Computers?" *School Library Journal* 47(10) (October 2001): 46.

2. Bruce Harley, Megan Dreger, and Patricia Knobloch, "The Postmodern Condition: Students, the Web, and Academic Library Services," *Reference Services Review* 29(1) 2001: 24.

3. Michael Gorman, "The Corruption of Cataloging," *Library Journal* (September 15, 1995): 34.

What do we, as a nation, care about books? How much do you think we spend altogether on our libraries, public or private, as compared with what we spend on our horses?

—John Ruskin, 1865

CHAPTER NINE

All We Need Is a Fast Horse: Riding Information Literacy into the Academy

William B. Badke

A popular government without popular information, or the means of acquiring it, is but a prologue to a farce or a tragedy, or perhaps both. Knowledge will forever govern ignorance, and a people who mean to be their own governors must arm themselves with the power which knowledge gives.

—James Madison

The teaching of information literacy (IL) has fallen on hard times. No, let me rephrase that: the teaching of bibliographic instruction/information literacy, after all these years, has yet to get off the ground. Many of us work at it with passionate intensity. But all of us are struggling to make IL anything more than the necessary evil that everyone except a librarian believes it to be. True, we now have the wonderfully detailed Association of College and Research Libraries (ACRL) "Information Literacy Competency Standards,"[1] with their high-blown call to develop lifelong learners by "incorporating information literacy across curricula, in all programs and services."[2] Accrediting bodies are getting on board and demanding that information-skills training be mandated in all schools under their care. But we know that where the rubber meets the tarmac, IL remains an underinflated tire.

We information-literacy instructors can be exciting, motivational, jolly as Santa after three glasses of champagne, and innovative to the point of winning a Master Teacher award, but most students, especially undergraduates, find us irrelevant and annoying. What is more, many professors figure we can do everything necessary for information literacy in a half-hour session—no, make that twenty-five minutes—so we can ram through two sections of the class in a one-hour lecture period. I scarcely need to provide evidence.[3] If you're teaching IL, the truth shouts at you every day.

So why do we go on crusading about this issue? Our students don't seem to want it. The rest of the faculty indicates little or no need for it.[4] Yet we keep asserting that this is the information age and no person who cannot acquire and make use of information efficiently and effectively can be considered educated. We push our way into classrooms and curricula with a message that almost nobody is interested in hearing—that our students don't know what to do with information, and, by gum, we're determined to teach them.[5]

The main reason we put ourselves through this continuous angst is that we really and truly believe in information literacy. We shake our heads daily as we watch the helpless state of hopeless students trying to do the impossible task of manipulating the vast world of information until it spits out the content that they need. They know how to use computers, but they couldn't recognize a controlled vocabulary if it bit them. They can spot an isolated fact a mile away, but they have no idea how to put that granule of data into context so that it makes sense and leads them to the rest of the pieces that would complete the puzzle. We can teach them how to use EBSCO, but we have to train them all over again when they turn to ProQuest. If ever there was a deficiency in higher education that deserved to be cause for a crusade, information illiteracy is it.

Our postmodern era has created a monster. His name is "information," and he's taken on the status of "that which makes the world go around." The problem is, we've let this creature build his own infra-structure without a whit of thought given to those who have to work with him. Everyone's so busy constructing better systems to handle in-formation that no one has the time or energy to make sure that people using them have any idea what to do. We all know that an information system is only as good as its retrieval capability, but we've neglected to do much of anything about the capabilities of the retrievers.

Consider Morris Goldstein's speech to the information industry in 1995:

> Today we publish databases that are merely strings of information records with little or no relationship to each other. Almost robotically we produce new databases, but we rarely try to put our products into the context of the user. We take them to the party, but don't seem to dance with them much. "Go to the journal . . . write an abstract . . . go to the next journal." We need to think about solving their information need in a broader sense than we have previously done.
>
> Most of us have not considered how our customers use our databases.[6]

If the industry is not paying much attention to users, who is? Enter academic librarians. We, more than any other group on earth, under-stand the most deadly of all secrets in modern society—that most peo-ple have no idea how to retrieve and use information properly, even when they appear to have all sorts of technological abilities. We know it, but the futility is that so few want to listen to us talk about it. Our fellow academics rarely observe students in the research process and thus assume that the dismal essays coming back to them are simply the norm. Students see us coming and (probably rightfully) assume we're about to unload one more "how to use this information gadget" lecture on them.

The lack of understanding in academia, the business world, and so-ciety in general is so profound that there will soon come a time when information systems will be so big and complicated that only a small elite will know how to retrieve anything useful from them. Sure, the experts prophesy convergence and single interfaces for multitudes of databases, but we know differently. If the database systems in your in-stitution are not many times more complicated this year than they were last year, you're in the midst of a funding collapse or you're not paying attention. A single interface for multiple databases won't work because every database is constructed by some evil genius who wants to put his or her own stamp on it, thus locking away crucial data to any but the specific search tools of that database. Merging databases into a single search is like putting your lunch in a blender and then trying to retrieve a potato chip—it may be in there, but you'll never find it.

Retrieval in itself isn't even the whole story. As Peter Lyman points out, simply getting data is only the beginning—now the user must have the skill to evaluate the quality of what has been retrieved in terms of whatever query began the search. This, as he argues, requires abilities akin to those of a reference librarian.[7]

And so the gap is ever widening between information systems built by people who value elegance over friendliness and the citizens of our modern world who care nothing about elegance and value only easy retrieval. This is no longer a problem for librarians. We're just the ones who noticed it first. This is a crisis for all of technological society. The data is going in, but fewer and fewer people know how to get it out.

During the Middle Ages, there was a similar gap. Most people were illiterate, and those who wrote and kept the books held the power. This also meant that the percentage of people in society who could truly make a creative contribution was small. That's why we call them the Dark Ages, and the current revisionist historians who are trying to find rays of light in those times are not succeeding very well.

The cure? Education. Literacy. Elevation of the intellectual gifts of the common man or woman. In the Renaissance, we saw not just a rebirth of the arts and humanities but a great broadening of the percentage of the population that knew how to read the books and, thus, could actually increase the likelihood of advancing the civilization.

Literacy is no longer as much of an issue even in the poorest countries of the world, but now we've changed the systems that once made literacy the answer to ignorance. Books were and still are the best information retrieval systems in the world. Computers are not. This is because you can browse a book. You can see its end from its beginning. You can explore every part of it as long as you have the simple gift of the ability to read. Computers, on the other hand, are black boxes. They are like libraries with closed stacks—you have to ask them for what you want, and a virtual library clerk looks all over until it finds a match, then retrieves what it thinks you asked for. If the clerk comes back without the data you wanted, you have no recourse but to go away empty handed or send the clerk on another potentially fruitless search.

Computers don't include everything, do they? We have hard copy all over the place so computers surely haven't replaced books and journals. But the fact is that they have replaced them, for the simple reason that any library of over a few hundred volumes requires a retrieval system, which almost universally these days is a computer. How many periodical indexes are still published in print form? Or indexes to government documents? The fact is that the primary interface between humans and the vast information holdings we've generated over all these centuries, hard copy or not, is the computer—the black box—only barely browsable and governed by ever more complicated search functions. Don't get me wrong. I love computers. The time we save and the kinds of amazing data searches we can do make computers invaluable in a time of rapid expansion of knowledge. Yet, I fear them for what they can do to us. No, not that they'll turn us into slaves or even kill off our ability to reason. My concern is deeper than that—I fear that computers will hold all the data eventually, and we'll lose the ability to get it back out. I'm afraid we're embarking on a new dark age of information illiteracy.

It wasn't such a problem when anyone who had graduated from elementary school could at least read hard-copy data in the form of books, journals, newspapers, and so on. But computer systems hide the data in devious ways, and complex skills are required to retrieve it. In a card catalog, if you had the spelling of an author's name wrong, you could likely do a bit of browsing and find what you needed in the same drawer or at least the next one. Ask a computer for data related to a misspelled name, and the computer tells you that the data does not exist. It's gone—forever. Unless you know how to search a controlled vocabulary or a browse list instead of using a simple keyword box, you'll never find it. As search programs increase in complexity, with guided searches and advanced searches and expert searches along with a zillion delimiters, clumsy hands will discover again and again the same words on the screen, "No results were found for your search query." Those eight words may well be our epitaph.

Obviously, though, I'm sounding like an extremist. Any fool with a computer can find at least something in a database. Search tools will never become so complex that only experts can retrieve any data at all. But the question is, how much disparity needs to exist between the complexity and size of systems and the skills of those who retrieve that data before retrieval simply doesn't work well enough to keep society functioning? Those of us who work the reference desk in academic institutions already know that most students—if pressed to find scholarly data on any given topic in, say, half an hour—either could not find enough or would present material that was inadequate in quality or relevance. Yet most of those very students will need to make their living handling information, the majority of it accessible only through complex computer systems.

If this is the problem, it begs for a solution. But if a solution is out there, it's awfully elusive. Despite the fact that bibliographic instruction and information literacy continue to be on the agenda, taught by creative and motivated people, most of our students graduate knowing little more than how to use the current version of our catalog and EBSCO, but only if pushed to do so. When they come back to us five or ten years down the road for graduate education, we'll have to teach them the new systems, which will look alien to them because they don't know how to transfer their understanding of one database to another.

After all this time, you wouldn't think we would be debating about the best method to teach information literacy or whether we should teach it at all. You don't find that kind of debate in the English department. What we are avoiding is the grim truth that virtually every attempt we make to turn information-literacy training into something viable falls on its face or ends up being considerably less than we'd hoped for.

We know that one-shot generic sessions aren't much good for long-term learning. Teaching done within specific courses provides some help in whatever discipline you're dealing with, but students make little transfer to other disciplines. Point-of-need instruction is great for motivation, but once again, students want answers only to their current problems and fail to transfer their knowledge to the next situation. Credit courses are hard to get into the curriculum and are usually attended only by the keenest students who least need the training. Making credit courses compulsory is next to impossible (though I've been fortunate to teach a compulsory one-credit course for the past seventeen years).

So what, then, is the answer? In my humble opinion, it is to get information literacy out of the library and into the academy. When I first came across "Information Literacy as a Liberal Art" by Jeremy J. Shapiro and Shelley K. Hughes,[8] I thought I'd finally found in print what I'd been thinking about for many years—that information-literacy education should not only join the liberal arts, but ought to become foundational to them. Shapiro and Hughes summed up their intent as follows:

> Information and computer literacy, in the conventional sense, are functionally valuable technical skills. But information literacy should in fact be conceived more broadly as a new liberal art that extends from knowing how to use computers and access information to critical reflection on the nature of information itself, its technical infrastructure, and its social, cultural, and even philosophical context and impact—as essential to the mental framework of the educated information-age citizen as the trivium of basic liberal arts (grammar, logic and rhetoric) was to the educated person in medieval society.[9]

But there's the rub. We're talking about introducing what amounts to a new discipline into the curriculum. Not only that, but we're seeing it as a generic offering supposedly foundational to all other programs, yet not at home in any of them. As such, it falls within the class of similar failed attempts to inject broad intellectual capacities into students, such as classical studies or logic and rhetoric (though public speaking as a skills course is flourishing). Consider this description of content from the Shapiro and Hughes proposal. After detailing several types of literacy demanded of their new discipline, they add one more that would demand superhuman effort to accomplish:

> Critical literacy, or the ability to evaluate critically the intellectual, human and social strengths and weaknesses, potentials and limits, benefits and costs of information technologies. This would need to include a historical perspective (e.g. the connection between algorithmic thinking, formalization in mathematics, and the development of Western science and rationality and their limits); a philosophical perspective (current debates in the philosophy of technology, the critique of instrumental reason,

the possibility and nature of artificial intelligence); a sociopolitical perspective (e.g. the impact of information technology on work, public policy issues in the development of a global information infrastructure); and a cultural perspective (e.g. current discussions of the virtual body and of the definition of human being as an information-processing machine).[10]

Compare this to the new ACRL Information Literacy Standards:

Information literacy . . . is an intellectual framework for understanding, finding, evaluating, and using information—activities which may be accomplished in part by fluency with information technology, in part by sound investigative methods, but most important, through critical discernment and reasoning. Information literacy initiates, sustains, and extends lifelong learning through abilities which may use technologies but are ultimately independent of them.[11]

The sheer workload demanded of any educational institution to accomplish all of this across the curriculum makes it a prime candidate for messy failure. Every administrator, every program director, every faculty member would have to be on the same page with the same motivation to promote information literacy as the new campus buzzword. To put it in another way, we would need to transform a single plow horse—our in-house IL classes—into a super enhanced war horse, even though it would be generic and, lack name recognition, and offer little to entice faculty to bet on it. Let's be realistic; it's not going to happen. Creating a new foundational discipline is a doomed enterprise. At best, accrediting bodies will force institutions to plug more information literacy into individual courses where it will continue to annoy both faculty and students alike. There simply is no strong will to make IL its own subject.

All this leaves us with a considerable amount of bad news. Traditional IL in the library setting, while likely doing some good, is a decidedly tough sell. "Point-of-need" and all the other current buzzwords may help somewhat, but students still seem almost never to develop a full set of skills transferable to any information need. And even to suggest that we trundle information literacy out into the academy as yet another "must have" discipline is likely as lost a cause as any other suggestion.

So is there a solution? Let me suggest one: a single, department-specific fast horse. Shapiro and Hughes weren't wrong, just overly ambitious. They failed to reckon with the harsh reality that a slightly lame plow horse is not going to metamorphose into a fierce warrior just because it plods into academia. What we need is a steed that is new enough and fast enough to be thrust into one part of the curriculum where we think it will fit and then to sell itself as a concept to the institution as a whole.

The strategy is this: we need to find a place in the curriculum for a new kind of information-literacy course that is not strongly tied to the library use but is geared to teaching students how to research and handle information in all its various forms in order to fulfill the educational outcomes of a particular university department.[12] The goal is not to produce a generic discipline for the whole academy but a single course, planned to meet the expectations for graduates of a selected department, but containing a core large enough to assure that students are literate with more broadly based information systems. The key is to demonstrate that a course in information literacy is integral to the success of the department with as much right to be there as is any other. Once it has proven its value, it can be replicated in other departments, not as a clone, but as a course that meets the particular needs of each department where it is offered—not course specific, but department specific.

Having just embarked on the process I'm about to describe, and having seen it succeed to the point of putting a course into the curriculum, I'm encouraged to suggest the following strategy, audacious as it may seem:

Step One: Cultivate a relationship (or pay attention to one you've already cultivated) with a department head in your institution who is both progressive and in charge of a department that is dynamic, innovative, and used to handling information. In my case, I already had a professor colleague who happened to have the right qualities and was chair of the communications department, so there was blessedly little to cultivate.

Step Two: If your library is not yet on board with your scheme, explain it to the colleagues who can make things happen. What you want is for them to release you to teach a three-credit course with some racy title like "Research in the Information Age." You want to offer it to a progressive department in your institution as a freebie. Chances are your own people are going to want to know why, and you'll tell them. In my case, our library director was ahead of me, and it was he who suggested we market it to the communications department as a gift from the library.

Step Three: Armed with a mandate from your library, approach the department head from Step One. Be very careful at this point. Everything must be put to him or her as an opportunity, which indeed it will be. Prepare yourself with a clear rationale as to why your research course will benefit the students in your friend's department. At no time mention libraries or term papers. This course is to be geared to further the educational aims of the department for which it is targeted, not particularly to keep the library happy or to provide students only with the skills they'll need while they're students. In my case, the communications department was a natural; they are educating journalists, media people, and so on—people who live and die by information. My approach was to say, if you teach communications, it's crucial that you offer a course in the methodology of acquiring and using information—a free course, by the way. If you've chosen well, your department-head friend will jump at the chance, as did mine.

Step Four: Push it through academic administration. Here's where the real work begins. You will have to overcome the following:

1. The perception that the institution already has information literacy through the library or course-specific add-ons, so a course like this is redundant. To answer, you need to be prepared to offer a radical shift in thinking. To this point, we have pitched information literacy as something analogous to driver training: Here is the car. You, the student, as the potential user of the car, need to be trained in its proper operation. When you are certified, you can drive it as it was intended to be driven.

   To meet goals of this kind, of course, I'm proposing actual work; you are going to have to cut the horse loose and let it run out into the academy alone. It is not an instructional program in library use (the driver-training model) but a dynamic adventure in learning how to acquire, evaluate, and otherwise handle information in an electronic environment within the parameters of the department in which it is located. The intent is not to teach students how to write better term papers but to be literate with information in its researching and manipulation demands, regardless of its format or origin. This is employment and life-skills training, not driver training. Students who do the course will be better fitted to take their place in the information revolution. Should they happen to learn about libraries on the way, as they surely will, that's nice. But learning about libraries is not the purpose, only one element in a much bigger picture.

2. Some administrators will justly say, "That's all we need—another skills course. This is an institution of higher learning, not a trade school."

Of course it is. That's why we will have theory as well as practice. But it will be "answering theory."

Let me explain. In my own discipline of theological studies, there are several ways to teach theology. One is to treat it as dogmatics, the word from on high, take it or leave it. In this approach, students are simply provided with the theory and are told that the application of it is more or less up to them. The opposite approach is an "answering theology," which starts with such basic human questions like, why am I here? and why is there evil? It then enlists the dogma to answer the questions. Theory becomes the handmaid to the problem being addressed.

Within the course you are proposing, you need to disguise the theoretical as "answering theory." Thus, a question like, why didn't my search work? becomes a lesson in Boolean theory and the distinctions between keywords and controlled vocabularies. A question like, why can't I get everything for free on the Net? becomes a teachable moment in the economics of information dissemination. All of this falls in line with the advice of Bruce Harley et al. that the postmodern student needs less to know about the workings of a particular database or the organizational structure of a library than how to think critically about information. An answering theory is intent on building a critical approach that facilitates the searching of many databases and the proper evaluation of results.[13]

You also need to make it clear that a course like this is not simply there to teach skills in isolation from method. Rather, all of the skills will be framed within a research strategy that allows the student to move from initial problem, through many forms of information gathering, to assessment of data collected, to final reshaping of information in answer to the initial problem. Without a strategic framework, the skills in themselves provide little benefit (which is why so many of our one-shot and point-of-need efforts fail).

3. An astute administrator may remark that this sounds like the sort of course everyone should take.

   Beware, despite the fact that this was something close to the plan all along—to infiltrate a research course into a key spot in one department, make it popular, and then allow its influence to spread through the institution until everyone wants his or her own department-specific version. But agreeing at this stage that everyone should take your course is a deadly trap for a couple of reasons:

   a. You do not have the personnel to offer the course to everyone, and until the whole campus really, really wants it, no one is going to provide more funding.

   b. You will find yourself under pressure to take the course out of the department in which you've cultivated it and call the thing a generic University Something-or-Other, where it will die for lack of sponsorship, rejected by students who view anything called University Something-or-Other as another plot to indoctrinate them with study skills. The genius of your approach has been that you've found an ideal home for such a course to catch on and become popular. If it is to be replicated, you want each version to have its own departmental spin so that it never reverts to the generic plow horse.

No one, except librarians and a scattering of faculty, sees much need for information literacy, despite the fact that we are rapidly moving toward a new dark age characterized by a lack of ability to retrieve and handle information in an electronic environment. Thus, we librarians need to launch information literacy into the academy as a new course offering, a fresh approach that has little "tincture of library" to it, but teaches students how to handle information needs within their own departmental parameters. If we teach it dynamically, in a department where learning such things makes sense, we can create a little jewel that others will want. The point of attraction is its relevance, something that a generic, foundational course offering or new discipline cannot demonstrate.

Trinity Western University's COMM 200: Research in the Information Age, began in January 2002—it was a calculated one. I believe it was a new beginning for us.[14]

Notes

1. Association of College and Research Libraries (ACRL), "Information Literacy Competency Standards for Higher Education" (2000), December 20, 2001. at www.ala.org/acrl/ilintro.html.

2. ACRL, "Information Literacy."

3. For some evidence of the difficulties, see Tom Eadie, "Immodest Proposals: User Instruction for Students Does Not Work," *Library Journal* 115 (October 1990): 42–45, and his "Beyond Immodesty: Questioning the Benefits of BI," *Research Strategies* 10 (Summer 1992): 105–10; Joanne Bessler, "Do Library Patrons Know What's Good for Them?" *Journal of Academic Librarianship* 16 (May 1990): 76–77. It is interesting to note that the most strident attacks on this enterprise came before the Internet and that the next generation of databases complicated our lives to a significantly greater extent. On the role of "less than entranced, or even hostile, clients" in academic teaching librarian burnout, see Deborah F. Sheesley, "Burnout and the Academic Teaching Librarian: An Examination of the Problem and Suggested Solutions," *Journal of Academic Librarianship* 27 (November 2001): 447–51.

4. See Gloria J. Leckie, "Desperately Seeking Citations: Uncovering Faculty Assumptions about the Undergraduate Research Process," *Journal of Academic Librarianship* 22 (May 1996): 201–8. Her argument is that faculty, as "expert researchers," have long since forgotten their undergraduate experience and approach the research process with vastly different assumptions than do their students, assumptions that minimize the perceived need for reference service and training. Edward K. Owusu-Ansah argues that faculty members' perceptions of librarians as constituting a lower order of academic life than themselves and of their institutional libraries as inferior also play a role. Edward K. Owusu-Ansah, "The Academic Library in the Enterprise of Colleges and Universities: Toward a New Paradigm," *Journal of Academic Librarianship* 27 (July 2001): 282–94.

5. Consider the bold and expensive initiatives of The Five Colleges of Ohio and Florida International University to make information a key element in as many courses as possible. Available at www.denison.edu/ohio5/grant and www.fiu.edu/~library/ili/iliprop.html (both accessed December 13, 2001).

6. Morris Goldstein, "Killer Apps: Miles Conrad Memorial Lecture, 1995," December 13, 2001, at www.pa.utulsa.edu/nfais/miles.d/1995.html. The polyanna approach of Verlene Herrington, who believes that all we need to do

is build simpler systems, flies in the face of the industry's motivation to make each product unique and with more features than competitors can offer: Verlene J. Herrington, "Way Beyond BI: A Look to the Future," *Journal of Academic Librarianship* 24 (September 1998): 381–86.

7. Peter Lyman, "Information Literacy," *Liberal Education* 87 (Winter 2001): 28–39.

8. Jeremy J. Shapiro and Shelley K. Hughes, "Information Literacy as a Liberal Art," *Educom Review* 31 (March/April 1996), December 9, 2001, at www.educause.edu/pub/er/review/reviewarticles/31231.html.

9. Shapiro and Hughes, "Information Literacy." See also Peter Lyman's rationale for information literacy as a liberal art, although he gives no clues as to how it could be implemented: Lyman, "Information Literacy."

10. Shapiro and Hughes, "Information Literacy."

11. ACRL, "Information Literacy" within the second subsection, "Information Literacy and Information Technology."

12. Such a concept isn't new. The following provide a few of the scattered examples of the use of such an approach, although its place in a larger strategy is not articulated: Marjorie M. Warmkessel and Joseph M. McCade, "Integrating Information Literacy into the Curriculum," *Research Strategies* 15 (Spring 1997): 80–88 (a graduate information-literacy course within an education department); Katherine B. Chiste et al., "Perspectives on Infiltration and Entrenchment: Capturing and Securing Information Literacy Territory in Academe," *Journal of Academic Librarianship* 26 (May 2000): 202–8 (creation of several courses within undergraduate departments of a university). For Scott Walter's website devoted to providing access to sample syllabi for such courses, see www.lib.ohio-state.edu/eduweb/sub.htm.

13. Bruce Harley et al., "The Postmodern Condition: Students, the Web, and Academic Library Services," *Reference Services Review* 29(1) (2001): 23–32.

14. For a copy of the syllabus go to www.acts.twu.ca/LBR/commsyll.htm.

Knowledge is the small part of ignorance that we arrange and classify.

—Ambrose Bierce

CHAPTER TEN

Information Literacy As Liberal Education: Academic Libraries, the Teaching Librarian, and Collection Marketing

Douglas M. Stehle

You must live feverishly in a library. Colleges are not going to do any good unless you are raised and live in a library every day of your life.

—Ray Bradbury

Does Bradbury's idea represent an operating principle in higher education today? Is such a deep connection between quality university education and library use necessary? Bradbury's statement raises philosophical questions about college education and academic libraries that are of the utmost importance as the academic library community considers the twenty-first century library and the future role of the librarian in higher education. Is information literacy the answer to the question of how reference and instruction librarians develop in the future and connect with student learning?[1]

Bradbury's point may sound somewhat outdated or anachronistic in the context of our new digital-information environment, but in essence, I think it nicely sums up our field's rationale for information literacy as that of serving the mission of quality education. But given this mission, are the current means proposed by the information-literacy movement within academic librarianship the best ones to achieve it? Is the current vision of information literacy as a curricular-teaching movement the right framework for organizing ourselves and our libraries to improve the education of the college undergraduate? The characteristics of the academic information-literacy movement—the focus on teaching students techniques, competencies, and skills; the fuzzy endorsement of information as our calling and expertise (over the wide word of knowledge in general); and the intense passion to establish librarians as teachers in particular curriculums working side-by-side with teaching faculty—do not strike me as the appropriate ways for librarians to position libraries for the future and best impact undergraduate learning.[2]

I suggest we reframe information literacy as something not to be taught or pedagogically engineered but as a rationale for libraries to more actively establish the presence of their collections on their campuses and to do so in ways that maximize the instruction librarian's time toward fostering the movement Bradbury is talking about. I believe this will encourage information literacy more broadly across the academic campus. A better way to secure the role of the academic reference/instruction librarian in supporting quality education is not through a transformation of library instruction (the current take on what information literacy is relative to the earlier era of bibliographic instruction) but through focusing our time on activities that more prominently display our collections to college students and define the library as the prime locus of liberal education on campus. Such an approach holds more promise for the academic library community in its effort at connecting with the mission to foster critical thinking and lifelong learning in the undergraduate college experience.

As we think about the ends and means of information literacy, we return to the real question, expressed by Bradbury: what makes up a quality college education? In other words, how should students spend their time intellectually during their college years, and what should the learning process look like? Bradbury's thought echoes many of today's buzz words—especially that of "lifelong learning"—used to talk about the ultimate aims of a university education, as well the aims of information literacy. That a student must read (Bradbury's living in the library), think (feverishly), and encounter discourse (again to live or to be raised in a library) during his or her college education (and beyond) to develop as a person strikes me as a fine statement that advocates both liberal education and information literacy. Information literacy strikes me as simply nothing more than the librarian's deep passion for liberal education. What concerns me is the path some advocate for involving ourselves with this mission.

Information Literacy and the Road to Damascus: Is Teaching the Way?

The current thinking centered around teaching techniques, enhanced bibliographic instruction, closer collaboration with teaching faculty, online tutorials, and special exercises (essentially more direct and formal teaching by librarians) will never bring about lifelong learning or liberal education. Information literacy is liberal education. I see information literacy as a cultural challenge, a challenge to the never-ending American ethos of anti-intellectualism and the utilitarian attack on liberal education.[3] As such, it cannot be approached from the level of reference and instruction services by bibliographic-instruction or teaching librarians. We are not dealing with fourth or fifth generation bibliographic instruction; we are moving beyond library instruction and heralding the death of a practice that has sown very little substantially. I am suggesting a return of focus to the centrality of reference librarianship, with a renewed emphasis on actively promoting our collections.

Only an institution—a social entity on the campus—that is, "the library" as whole, can solve what instruction librarians have identified, quite rightly, as the problem. The problem is the absence of intellectually rigorous liberal education; information literacy seeks to renew liberal education. I think this has become blurred or buried underneath our rubrics and jargon. We have begun to turn the corner toward competencies, standards, and outcome assessment, and we risk leaving behind that which is the soul of librarianship once and for all. If a quality education is about liberal education taking hold and fostering lifelong learning, then students need to be exposed to an active center that speaks the various languages of liberal education. This means collection marketing. Librarians (who else?) need to do this with their libraries—their true teaching spaces.

The library at a college or university does not merely serve one academic department. It serves them all via collections that span the broad-ranging field of human knowledge and inquiry. Taken as a whole, the library is not about subdisciplines; it is about the entire body of knowledge and the potential that knowledge offers to those who seek an education. The library in and of itself is liberal education embodied through its collections, especially if we engender use of the collections among undergraduates. Information literacy should be read as a broad philosophy of academic librarianship and not a narrow articulation of the pedagogical dynamics on the part of the teaching librarian. I suspect that this latter rendering serves the identity crisis, which never ceases to plague us, of "librarian— or something better?" We need to recognize that our curriculum is right in our own house, that our classroom is the library, and that no mediator need stand between us and the general student whom we wish to introduce to the possibilities our collections represent.

Consciously or not, the library community has put itself in the middle of the pedagogical wars, and we need to realize that information literacy is less about process and technique and more about the ends of education. Information literacy is indeed a pedagogy in the broadest of terms that puts forth a vision of how colleges "can do some good." Simple examples of this are evident in conference gatherings or electronic discussion lists where someone eventually declares the obvious: working with faculty is not the answer; we need our own curriculum to promote information literacy. But this is an answer on the small and somewhat idealistic level. Making information literacy another "discipline" in the already bloated and fragmented curriculum is a bad idea and will probably make things worse. The grand majority of libraries and librarians will not and cannot offer a curriculum on their campuses for the obvious reasons of economic, political, psychological, and resource limitations. While we talk about "collaboration with teaching faculty" as the way to integrate the library across the curriculum, we seem to be in denial over how the idea of the "teaching librarian" is a direct challenge to the power over pedagogy possessed by the very faculty with whom we wish to collaborate. How many of the teaching faculty collaborate successfully in the same course in higher education? If you agree with me that 90 percent of teaching faculty do not recognize librarians as "teachers, like them," and that academic teaching space is a political zone we can't just waltz into, then we have to reengineer how to carry out the lofty goal of information literacy.

My point is that the current means of information literacy eventually cancel out its noble ends. Those in leadership positions must begin to recognize this and shift the focus of their library-instructional staffs, who overestimate the potential outcomes and impact of the collaborative, integrated, teaching mode. Idealism is a wonderful motivating tool, but to allow our idealism about information literacy as a movement of "the teaching librarian" to blind us to the unrealistic and unlikely success of this on most academic campuses is a disservice to our users, our campuses, and in the long run, to ourselves. Information literacy should become a movement about liberal education, not teaching students about this, that, and some other competency. In this revaluation of information literacy, the librarian's teaching space is the library and not the curriculum. Our content or subject expertise is the collections (not information skills[4] and the "how to" with this piece and that), and our efforts should be toward making students intensely aware of the content of library collections outside the curriculum.

The ends of information literacy are not being called into question. I do, however, propose an expansion of our understanding of those ends in order to reshape how instruction librarians connect with quality college education, student learning, and liberal education. The problem becomes, how do we implement our connection to maximize the true ends? Specifically, what should "instruction librarians" or "information-literacy librarians" spend their time on? Should our means be the same as the teaching faculty? Can this be the right direction, given the structure most academic librarians exist within? Should we continue to try to collaborate with a group that really does not see us as equals and has its own agenda at heart—an agenda that does not insure that undergraduates receive a good general dose of library collections? The problem the academic library community has faced for so long is working with (or against?) teaching methods that reduce library use to a mere retrieval technique, while at the same time desiring to impart to the student the idea that the library is much more than this.

On Liberal Education and Libraries

> The notion of the free play of the mind upon all subjects being a pleasure in itself, being an object of desire, being an essential provider of elements without which a nation's spirit . . . must, in the long run, die of inanition. . . . But criticism, real criticism [liberal education], is essentially the exercise of this very quality. It obeys an instinct prompting it to try to know the best that is known and thought in the world, irrespectively of practice, politics, and everything of the kind.
>
> —Matthew Arnold[5]

What is liberal education? For "liberal," I suggest the dictionary definition of "originally, the distinctive epithet of those 'arts' or 'sciences' that were considered 'worthy of a free man' . . . directed to general intellectual enlargement and refinement."[6] Liberal education is about cultivating humanity. Martha Nussbaum, writing about citizenship and education, refers to the Greek and Roman ideas of "an education that is 'liberal' in that it liberates the mind from the bondage of habit and custom, producing people who can function with sensitivity and alertness as citizens of the whole world." She concludes that Seneca's favored version of an education that is *liberalis* can serve us well today: "an education is truly fitted for freedom only if it is such as to produce free citizens, citizens who are free . . . because they can call their minds their own."[7]

College education should be about liberal education. It should foster the individual's craving for freedom in learning, and to do this, it must provide an environment that promotes events leading to this inculcation. Librarians introduce students to collections that provide and even embody the liberal quest for knowledge. The library and its collections are the greatest assemblage of parts, and a whole greater than those parts that together provide for liberal education awareness and its development of the openly critical spirit alluded to by Matthew Arnold. I believe we can reach more students through collection marketing than through instruction programs to accomplish this.

Information literacy should be developed as a framework for modeling our library practice in ways that symbolize the broader goals of liberal education and that work to foster rigor, student engagement, and lifelong learning. Information literacy ought to be less about what, if, and how librarians teach students and more about how we connect our collections to potential readers, to potential feverish minds. Does the current race toward teaching savvy accomplish our true intent and encourage students to live among us, among the books? Who are we and how do we finally reach our goals in peace? (And no one need accuse me of being romantic here; books come in many formats, and while I think part of information literacy should be about books, I do not mean only the "printed" book per se.)

Living feverishly in a library means one thing and one thing only: reading.[8] One certainly does not need to live in a library today to surf the Web since this can be done at home, from coffeehouses, or from any decent computer lab on campus. Libraries must be about more than just getting information and evaluating it for problem-solving purposes and job preparation. Students can also study anywhere and can read the assigned reading spoon-fed via course reserves. Why would they want to live in a library? What else lives there that is an essential ingredient of a good college education? No, not librarians. Simply put, books. Books and the knowledge they contain. It might follow, then, that Bradbury is saying that without reading, college education is lost. Is information literacy about reading? Perhaps, but if not, we should make it so.

Information literacy, I hope, is a call to return to reading and the book. I do not mean the physical book per se, but the book as catalyst of that quest for knowledge that is liberal education, the kind of education due a free person, a free thinker. The ideas one needs to interact with to fully become fully free, to acquire one's worldview in the space of liberal education, are best discovered through books. As libraries are warehouses of books (something we should not be ashamed of), they are thus warehouses of knowledge. Living in a library is the realization of liberal education, the feverish road to getting more from college than a degree. By "return to the book," I mean a commitment to thinking and reading.[9]

Collection Marketing and Teaching Space

The lack of access to traditional teaching space, the lack of authority to create and control curricular space, the inability to share that access with those faculty members who do not want to share, means that trying to access learners in specific curricular areas is a dead end and will never succeed on a significant level or to an extent that makes it worth our efforts, resources, and identity. The mediators between us and students, who do seem to embrace us at times, still never quite speak our language, nor does their language allow our words of liberal education through our collections to pass freely through their specialist concerns. Ours is the language of the generalist, the liberal generalist; theirs is the language of the specialist. We are joined, we are related, but we should not become one, nor seek to become them.

Lack of access to students by academic librarians demonstrated the need to evolve the teaching librarian's role. Perhaps most instruction should be halted and the time devoted to collection display, marketing and promotion of selected item sets week by week, reading promotion, and intense bibliography disseminations. We will certainly take time to contact and discuss assignment problems with instructors when we encounter their students adrift, but we should not invite classes for instruction sessions as some sort of solution. At most, the majority of undergraduate library instruction ought to be eliminated in favor of faculty training. If we must teach, if we must see teaching as a means to information literacy, then let it be something that fosters empowers the teaching faculty to teach with the collections that we alert it to. Let us make those who do have the access, the power, and control over student directions somewhat more information literate and hope for the best.

Instruction librarians should begin to see the library collections—large chunks of ideas—as their material, the entire library space—floor-by-floor, wall-by-wall—as their classroom, and library events that present, reveal, and promote these chunky ideas as teaching times. All undergraduates are our students with the potential of becoming co-dwellers in communion with the richness of liberal learning that our collections resonate with and represent. Surround the entire campus with a collection presence that serves the large mission and do so on our own, quietly, without asking for effort on the faculty's part—they are busy, too, and probably too busy to integrate with us. Then, watch the library invade the curriculum from the outside, instead of trying to ice skate uphill by working with faculty and particular programs on the inside. Most of us are limited in terms of how much we can support, how many sessions and departments we can "integrate" with. Instead of controlling a fifty-minute bibliographic-instruction session, control the space that is ours: the library space. Instead of pouring vast amounts of time and energy into a course-related program with the hope that retention and transfer will occur with that particular group, target all interested and potential liberal learners with the collections that we are truly expert in.

Perhaps we avoid this because if over use were to really become an issue, librarians might have to face up to the inability of our libraries to accommodate it. All of us see this in planning sessions considering new programs or enhancing old ones—a consistent theme in many a committee meeting is the red herring question of, what if we get hordes of people coming at us who actually want to make use of this? is a consistent theme in many a committee meeting. It is amazing that, after Ernest Boyer's study of the undergraduate experience in college, the academic library community did not make increasing use the number-one priority.[10] We have turned down a dark path and are on a narrow ridge. It is time for a reality check. Our rich heritage and love of bibliography only need the drama, theatre, and energy of the instruction librarian to curate the library collections into an intellectual showcase for the campus. Just as the holy "reference interview" was overcome, so we must now overcome mystic "integrated collaboration of the teaching librarian."

The current problem with the information-literacy movement is that it tries to root out individual discovery of the power of libraries (or reading?) and somehow translate that into a curriculum, as something that can be mediated and engineered by the librarian pedagogue. Our field seems intent on following suit (somewhat late, however) with the university tendency toward discrete specialization and technical training in specific techniques over that of an emphasis on solid general education for our undergraduates. The current urge amongst some instruction librarians to push for stand-alone information-literacy courses and even full-fledged curriculums clearly illustrate our profession's foray into this savage garden—one replete with the prized academic flower of the star teacher. While this chapter is not intended to address the professional dynamics of the situation, one wonders to what extent such items as the need for faculty-like status, prestige, salary, professionalism, and the many additional degrees held by some librarians factor into the inclinations of those pushing for the full-fledged emergence of the teaching librarian, a librarian concerned with the techniques of pedagogy and the specifics of information handling—a specialist—a legend in our own minds!

Why is this a problem? Because I do not believe it can be done. I do not know this, but it is a passionate belief I have after many years in the academic library scene, in reference and instruction, with plenty of first-hand work (and honest negotiations) with the teaching faculty I've served. It is a matter of first principles and how the program emerging from one's primary assumption effectively impacts the situation. The first principle being embraced by information-literacy enthusiasts seems to be that the academic library community can teach its way into becoming central to the university of the future. The librarian as instructional collaborator is seen by many as the best mode for librarians to foster lifelong education. My concern with such a principle is the depth and reach of the programs emerging from this rhetoric. Are information-literacy strategies all that much of an evolution beyond "older" bibliographic-instruction modes? What percentage of academic library-instruction programs have moved beyond the framework of the one-shot, fifty-minute session? How many collaborative programs can library-instruction operations provide for across the curriculum? Should budding instruction librarians feel pressure to offer such programs? Has information literacy given us much beyond new jargon that has changed the core of a good course-integrated plan between librarian and instructor? I do not see the money and resources or response from our co-collaborators (the teaching faculty) rising anywhere near the tidal wave proportions necessary to implement the new curriculum as envisioned and framed by the latest definitions and standards. I am not convinced that even a strong minority of teaching faculty or university administrators see librarians as the bedrock of a new curriculum for their campuses.[11] Turning our attention away from the promotion of our collections (which is our expertise) to teaching students the specific skill sets we call information literacy—often including the application and ethical issues of information in which most practitioners are not experts—seems not only naïve, but dangerous.

For all the thousand digital points of success along the way in this "new era" of library instruction, I still sense tremendous burnout and ultimate dissatisfaction on the part of practicing instruction librarians in terms of their ability to establish the library and themselves as pedagogues on their campus. Have bibliographic-instruction burnout and the instruction "blahs" been overcome by information literacy?[12] Perhaps I speak for a minority of library-instruction practitioners who realize that we have carved a path of Sisyphus for ourselves in our bid to become central sages of teaching excellence in higher education. Much of this goes to the heart of the paradigmatic battle that I would claim underlies many of the tensions in academic librarianship, especially reference and instruction circles: to be proactive or not, or to sit and wait for the patron's question or to go out and create our interaction with patrons. The drive of the instruction community to become pedagogues and instructional experts begins with the choice not to sit idly by and wait for requests for "tours."[13] This choice was the right choice, has the right intent, and bears the same spirit that our definition of information literacy as liberal education does. But I would rather direct this energy in different ways and channel it toward other activities for the instruction librarian that have little to do with the past of bibliographic-instruction sessions, one-shots, demos, lectures, tours, and the like. Our best chance for becoming recognized as essential in the process is to de-emphasize our obsession with teaching and establish our presence as collection advocates. An area for further pursuit and development is to articulate such collection marketing techniques and modes of production as means for approaching the implementation of information literacy.

What do students see when they enter our library? What do they encounter at each corner and nook, on each floor and wall? Are the possibilities of our collections modeled before their eyes? An ancient Stoic once said that we covet what we see; the eye shapes the mind. How are we presenting our collections to the eyes and minds of college undergraduates? To live in the library means that the library is a home. We must make it the home of liberal education for the entire campus—students and faculty—who wish to find that home. But the home must be visible and inviting. I advocate fewer tours, less library instruction per course, and fewer information-literacy exercises. Information-literacy librarians (a.k.a. reference and/or instruction librarians) need to become as the "curators" of the library as a "museum" of living ideas, actively taking the collections, presenting them to readers, and highlighting how they not only relate to each other but how they obviously connect to the inquiry and education that is the right of the reader.

Attracting users to the library for its intellectual promise and potential, for its comforts of a liberal home, is the strategy best suited to achieve the mission. I do not want to address the luxuries of libraries, such as coffee shops, study space and group rooms, quiet nooks, wood grain, and the rest, but those items should not be criticized solely owing to their supposed commercial origins or crass simplistic aims. It is not a bastardization of the realm of libraries to work toward morphing into bookstores; it is also about the entire culture of the quiet mind studying the book—the liberal mind freely thinking and engaged in a beautiful space. But beyond the wall coverings and wood grain must lay the presentation of intense and connected knowledge. We should hang on to our wood-grain walls reminders of what lies inside our building. Library staff and time need to be specifically devoted to daily, weekly, monthly, and annual showcases of the collections and the knowledge they represent. Cut your instruction program in half, increase your book displays by 50 percent. I am not saying we should be mere keepers of the book; we should be active presenters of our collections, which hold the real key to the discovery of learning.

Developing library activities and enabling mechanisms to promote liberal education serve as the operational goal of libraries seeking to implement information literacy on their campuses. The teaching librarian's role, as it is articulated currently, and the emphasis on teaching—whether through enhanced one-shots or collaborative integrations beyond bibliographic instruction—should be abandoned. Instilling and fostering the fever of lifelong learning, which is the ultimate goal of liberal education, is what information literacy should work toward. Once that fever infects, we have space in which patron and reference librarian can relate—the teachable moment, the learning opportunity self-directed by the person who has chosen to make sure his or her college experience does some good.

Final Reflection: Either/Or Hegelian Style

What strikes me as so powerful about Bradbury's quote is the individualistic essence of his point, the emphasis on the "you," or thus, the "I": "You must live feverishly in a library. Colleges are not going to do any good unless you are raised and live in a library everyday of your life." I think the library-instruction community needs now, more than ever before, to embrace the individualistic nature of the passion for knowledge and the individual choice that is the true motivator for all that follows after. Instead of emphasizing the pieces of the research process and stressing the competencies of information management, we ought to stress and promote what libraries are in the first place and design the information-literacy activities that promote liberal education.

Bradbury does not say "students"; he does not even say "people." And while I'm sure he knew some wonderful librarians and understood our value, he does not need to mention us, because it is the individual at stake—the reader. "You must live feverishly in a library"; colleges are not going to do any good unless students are raised and live in the library in body and in spirit. Certainly the social allusion evident in the word "raised" would imply that an elder is present, that interaction is afoot, and possibly that a Martin Buber–like I–Thou relationship is essential.[14] But somehow this does not overcome the emphasis of the "you." Ultimately, a quality college education is a matter of individual choice, will, and motivation on the part of the learner. Once that choice is made, then library use is crucial to the experience of a sound college education—use of the collections, browsing, scanning, reading, engaging the diversity of thought on the issues introduced by the collections. What are we doing to make that choice happen?[15]

The radical democracy, freedom, and liberal education that library collections provide cannot be addressed, distilled, or delivered by the current means being employed by the information-literacy movement.

But in the end, such is the ultimate goal of information literacy. We should worry less about teaching, less about programs of instruction, and instead take the energy and skills of reference and instruction librarians and point them in the direction of intense marketing and promotion of the ideas, events, people, themes, and human problems our collections represent. We should implement as many activities of shaping the interior landscape of the library in ways that attract and generally enlighten potential readers as we provide instructional sessions for the specific information tasks of users. I wonder if both can be done, and if not, then which is more important. Which mode best allows librarians to claim that we are fostering the beginning of a quality undergraduate education that lasts a lifetime? This is your choice.

One may glean from all this a question about the relation between reference and instruction librarians. Around the time of the critical analysis of the mystified reference interview,[16] the instruction community arose and took precedence over the mainstay of its past. But now the rhetoric of information literacy waxes so idyllic about the teaching librarian that the time is again ripe to shift forward and remold the reference librarian as something else; I propose as "collection promoter." Perhaps this is nothing more than renewed selective dissemination of information; it depends on how willing we are to realign our time, resources, and roles on our campuses. I would rather not think that it is a matter of reference versus instruction, but such questions about relations, roles, and the efficacy of each are not new. [17] We must retain the outgoing spirit of the instruction librarian in our recast, but with a reality check as to what librarians have to offer of real value to the academic community: the library, its collections, and liberal education.

Notes

1. I have taken great liberty with the many grand generalizations I make in this chapter. I ignore the variety of institutional missions, settings, and resources on different campuses. I decided to let the pen flow and share those deepest of private thoughts that have occurred to me over the past eight years. For five years, I coordinated a hectic and intense library-instruction program at Pittsburg State University in Kansas. There, in a four-year institution (about 7,000 FTE) with a staff of twelve librarians, I typically delivered at least eighty

of the program's 100 or more instruction sessions per fall and spring terms. Over the years, I have read widely, mixed it up on the discussion lists, and attended state and national conferences (LOEX of the west, the Institute for Information Literacy, etc.). As I have read and listened to my colleagues, perused the many excellent library websites with mission statements and projects promoting information literacy, I've always tried to bring it all back down to my own experience of managing and servicing requests from faculty for library orientation. On the basis of this experience and exposure to the broader practices and philosophies of today's current library-instruction field, I wrote this piece, letting it go where it had to. Hopefully, there is a nugget here, a reasonable question there, and even a subjective insight into objective truth somewhere in this postmodern quagmire—my little rant on information literacy.

2. There is a great deal of literature on information literacy. I highly recommend the introductory matter of *Objectives for Information Literacy Instruction: A Model Statement for Academic Librarians*, approved by the ACRL board January 2001 and available from their Standards & Guidelines area online at www.ala.org/acrl/guides/index.html. Currently, see Wenxian Zhang, "Building Partnerships in Liberal Arts Education: Library Team Teaching," *Reference Services Review* 29 (2001): 141. The entire number-two issue of *Reference Services Review* from 2001 is a testament to this trend. In this issue, one also finds forward-thinking Christine Bruce, whom I admire because she does not hold back in regard to the utilitarian and commercial aspects of her version of information literacy; librarians should and do collaborate with teaching faculty to deliver "lifelong learning and *associated graduate capabilities* [my emphasis]" by teaching information skills. I'm not sure Bruce's "lifelong learning" is my lifelong learning, and I find cause for alarm in the abstract to her article that defends the information literacy needs of students against the more "narrow focus on using the library and its information resources." Use of the library by readers is something that I see as totally necessary for sound liberal education; broad general use of its resources is necessary to find the best of what has been known and to cultivate one's humanity, as I argue in this chapter (see notes 6 and 8).

3. Bruce S. Thornton, "The Twilight of the Professors," *Bonfire of the Humanities: Rescuing the Classics in an Impoverished Age*, eds. Victor David Hanson, John Heath, and Bruce S. Thornton (Wilmington, Del.: ISI Books, 2001), 303. While I tend to be more liberal than the authors of this book, who go too far in their defense of the conservative position as represented by Allan Bloom, I do think they are correct in their comparison of the liberal education views of Bloom and Martha Nussbaum. For a librarian sage on this point, read Brian Quinn's "The McDonaldization of Academic Libraries?" *College & Research Libraries*, 61(3) (2000): 248–62.

4. "Throughout the 25 year period, academic librarians developed the concept of user instruction from library orientation to library instruction to course-integrated user instruction to information skills instruction." In Hannelore B. Rader, "A Silver Anniversary: 25 Years of Reviewing the Literature Related to User Instruction," *Reference Services Review* 28(3) (2000): 290–96.

5. Matthew Arnold, "The Function of Criticism at the Present Time," *Culture and Anarchy and Other Writings*, ed. Stefan Collini (Cambridge: Cambridge University Press, 1993), 35–36.

6. *Oxford English Dictionary*, 2d ed., s.v. "liberal.".

7. Martha C. Nussbaum, *Cultivating Humanity: A Classical Defense of Reform in Liberal Education* (Cambridge, Mass.: Harvard University Press, 1997), 8–9, 293–94.

8. William H. Wisner, *Whither the Postmodern Library?: Libraries, Technology, and Education in the Information Age* (Jefferson, N.C.: McFarland & Co., 2000): 72–73. Broader yet, but a fantastic read, is Alvin Kernan, *In Plato's Cave* (New Haven, Conn.: Yale University Press, 1999), specifically chapter 12, "The New Technology Calls All in Doubt."

9. Thomas Mann, *The Oxford Guide to Library Research* (New York: Oxford University Press, 1998), xv. Mann provides an excellent preface that addresses format and what he calls a hierarchy of learning, giving special attention to the format of the book for carrying "higher levels of thought."

10. Ernest L. Boyer, *College: The Undergraduate Experience in America* (New York: Harper & Row, 1987), 160–61; chapter ten was devastating, to me at least. How sure are we that things are any better; or are they worse? At times, when listening to information-literacy advocates speak about collaborative integration and their teaching role, one wonders if they even care. Have we lost Ranganathan's healthy focus on book and reader and opted to focus on ourselves more?

11. Have D. W. Farmer's "barriers to implementation" been overcome? I am especially interested to know to what extent the faculty barriers which Farmer so eloquently laid out have been offset or remedied. See D. W. Farmer, "Information Literacy: Overcoming Barriers to Implementation," *New Directions for Higher Education 78, Information Literacy: Developing Students as Independent Learners* (San Francisco: Jossey-Bass, 1992), 104–7. Call me the skeptic, but I am not sure that these barriers have been eliminated in significant ways on a majority of campuses.

12. Michelle Cash Russo, "Recovering from Bibliographic Instruction Blahs," *RQ* 32 (Winter 1992): 178–83; Karen A. Becker, "The Characteristics of Bibliographic Instruction in Relation to the Causes and Symptoms of Burnout," *RQ* (Spring 1993): 346–57.

13. A nasty little word that is still used heavily by those "un-hip" faculty when they should be requesting a collaborative integrated information-literacy experience espoused by us higher librarian types. Ignoring my sarcasm, the word does persist in practice and this is known by all practicing instruction co-ordinators.

14. Martin Buber, *I and Thou*, trans. Walter Kaufmann (New York: Scribner, 1970).

15. "The whole idea of a library is based on a misunderstanding: that a reader goes to the library to find a book whose title he knows. . . . The essential function of a library is to discover books of whose existence the reader had no idea" (Umberto Eco). Collection marketing is about helping to make this essential function occur to a much greater extent; I view "information skills" oriented information literacy as serving mostly the misunderstanding that Eco points out.

16. Lisa L. Smith, "Evaluating the Reference Interview: A Theoretical Discussion of the Desirability and Achievability of Evaluation," *RQ* 31 (Fall 1991): 75–77. Smith's article is not focused on deconstructing the reference interview; her article evaluates the reference interview in theory and practice. But her early paragraphs do seem to demystify the holier than thou perspective sometimes associated with reference and its once prominent act of the interview. In either case, the article appeared right about the time the mystification of library instruction into information literacy by academic librarians had begun to take off and develop to where we are at today.

17. James Rettig, "The Convergence of the Twain or Titanic Collision? BI and Reference in the 1990s' Sea of Change," *Reference Services Review* 23 (Spring 1995): 7–20.

I go into my library, and all history unrolls before me. I breathe the morning air of the world while the scent of Eden's roses yet lingered in it, while it vibrated only to the world's first brood of nightingales, and to the laugh of Eve. I see the pyramids building; I hear the shoutings of the armies of Alexander.

—Alexander Smith

CHAPTER ELEVEN

From Library-College
to Information Literacy:
An Evolving Strategy for
Educating Library Users

Jon R. Hufford

When a college is a library and a library is a college, it is a library-college.

—Louis Shores

On January 10, 1989, the American Library Association's (ALA) Presidential Committee on Information Literacy (the state of being an educated information consumer) issued its report on information literacy, thus initiating the library profession's goals of developing

> in each citizen a sense of his or her responsibility to acquire knowledge and deepen insight through better use of information and related technologies; [of instilling] a love of learning, a thrill in searching, and a joy in discovering; and [of teaching] young and old alike how to know when they have an information need and how to gather, synthesize, analyze, interpret, and evaluate the information around them.[1]

Following the publication of this report, the idea of information literacy for everyone flourished within the profession and has become one of its hottest topics, evoking numerous workshops, seminars, discussion forums, and published articles. Surely all ALA members know about the information-literacy initiative, and most members are probably familiar with the philosophy and general principles underlying information literacy. What most librarians may not be aware of is information literacy's long-standing pedigree. The philosophy and basic tenets of information literacy are not the newborn progeny of individuals who, stimulated by the phenomenal growth of computer technology and the Internet in recent years, experienced a sudden flash of genius that led to several new ideas they defined with a new term. On the contrary, these ideas have a time-honored past that significantly adds substance and validity to the information-literacy initiative.

Information literacy has replaced, or is in the process of replacing, terms such as "bibliographic instruction" and "library instruction," which defined an earlier kind of training in research techniques or strategies centered on the use of printed resources. As a matter of fact, the tenets of information literacy have been discussed, written about, and supported, either officially or unofficially, by the ALA and the Association of College and Research Libraries (ACRL) since the 1930s. In every field of human interest, the terms used to define ideas change over time. New developments in the technology that are in some way related to the ideas impact the choice of terms and even alter the way the terms are understood. This is what happened to bibliographic instruction as it evolved over the recent decades into what we now call information literacy. What stands out in this process is the consistency of the guiding ideas of instruction in library use, especially beginning in the 1950s and 1960s when Louis Shores's ideas for a library-college were first discussed in the professional literature.

Beginnings of a Strategy

In the very first issue of *Library Journal* in 1876, Melvil Dewey set the philosophical basis for librarians to teach people how to use the library and how to educate themselves.[2] He declared that "the largest influence over the people is the printed page, and that this influence may be yielded most surely and strongly through our libraries." Dewey went on to say that the librarian

> must put every facility in the way of readers, so that they shall be led on from good to better. He must teach them how, after studying their own wants, they may themselves select their reading wisely. Such a librarian will find enough who are ready to put themselves under his influence and direction, and, if competent and enthusiastic, he may soon largely shape the reading, and through it the thought, of his whole community.

He concluded his article by maintaining that

> the time was when a library *was* very like a museum, and a librarian was a mouser in musty books, and visitors looked with curious eyes at ancient tomes and manuscripts. The time is when a library *is* a school, and the librarian is in the highest sense a teacher, and the visitor is a reader among the books as a workman among his tools.

Librarians have found this philosophical basis for their role in education valid throughout the years. And it still is today.

Not surprisingly, it was nineteenth-century academicians who advocated formal education in library use—a trend that continues to this day. Articles written by authors as diverse as the philosopher Ralph Waldo Emerson, federal higher education official Kendric Babcock, and academic librarian Azariah Smith Root began to appear promoting credit courses in "bibliography." Louis Shores, another academician, was the most important leader of the twentieth-century library-instruction movement. He wrote several articles over four decades discussing his ideas for a "library-college."

The Library-College Idea

At the ALA convention held in Chicago in 1934, Shores read a paper entitled "The College of Library Arts." This paper spurred the beginning of the library-college movement. Shores proposed that classroom-centered group teaching be replaced by library-oriented, independent study. He defined the faculty person's role in this new learning mode as that of a counselor. He also suggested, in recognition of the growing importance of audio-visual materials in the 1930s, that the printed page was no longer the only educational resource. Further, he sketched a design for a "library-college" library where each student had his exclusive study desk at which he worked regular hours while attending class only when he felt the need to. The paper prompted considerable discussion. Much of the opposition came from academic librarians who supported the traditional idea that academic librarians only supported the classroom and should not be involved in teaching.[3]

Later Shores's ideas for the library-college were more clearly defined in the Jamestown Charter, a document named after the Jamestown College Workshop held in North Dakota in December 1965. The charter maintained that the purpose of the library-college was to enhance student learning through the use of library-centered independent study, with a bibliographically expert faculty person available for mentoring. The faculty person's role in the library-college was to enhance the student's independent study primarily through bibliographic counseling. Shores described bibliographic counseling as the sensitive matching of individual differences in students with individual differences in media." Though bibliographic counseling was to be the main role of the library-college faculty, the traditional functions of lecturing and research would not be eliminated. Instead, the library-college was to reinforce "faculty creativity by releasing the instructor from much of the classroom lockstep." Shores saw librarians as ideal bibliographic counselors who could fill the role even more effectively than teaching faculty.

Another important aspect of the library-college was the concept of the "generic book." This included printed, audio-visual, and computer-based materials used to educate students. As book production began to be augmented by audio-visual and computer-assisted formats in the 1950s and 1960s, it became possible to custom-tailor communication to the individual needs and abilities of the student population. Shores believed that it was just as valid to educate students using films, sound recordings, or computers as it was to use printed books. Distance learning, lifelong learning, and work-study also had important roles to play in his vision for a library-college.

The model curriculum that was developed at the Jamestown Workshop required "generalia" areas at the beginning of a student's education. One proposed course in this theoretical curriculum, titled "Information

Retrieval," required an education in "knowing how to find out." It was to be a "library-instruction course extraordinary" compared with the typical freshman library orientation many colleges and universities have offered for years. The other required generalia course in this theoretical curriculum was titled "Knowledge" and would have provided a broad overview of all knowledge. From then on, the curriculum was to move from the general to the specialized. At the end, there would be a return to a capstone synthesis of everything learned.

Shores believed that the librarian knew better than any faculty colleague how to find knowledge; however, he thought that the library profession needed to revitalize instruction in library use. For one thing, he wanted instruction in the use of resources to include the whole range of media, including print, audio-visual, microform, and computer technology. But more than that, he believed that academic librarians had to find new ways to teach library instruction and that higher education needed to allocate greater prominence to this subject. Incidentally, he felt that a new generation of college faculty was fundamental to the success of the library-college. He may well have thought the same way about librarians.

Another development in the field of higher education during these early years lent support to some of Shores's library-college ideas. In 1940, the Association of American Colleges was awarded a Carnegie grant to investigate college teaching in the United States. This investigation led to the publication of a book authored by Harvie Branscomb, chancellor at Vanderbilt University. *Teaching with Books* revealed how poorly most faculty used books and libraries in their teaching. It also criticized the traditional academic librarian's often self-imposed supporting role in the educational process. Branscomb went on to challenge academic librarians to come up with an educational dimension for their profession.

The Bibliographic-Instruction Movement

Academic librarians did in fact begin a movement to revitalize library instruction. Patricia Knapp developed a program of bibliographic instruction that owed much to Shores's ideas. It was piloted at Wayne State University's experimental Monteith College in the early 1960s.

Knapp's subsequent report on the pilot study and her revised model program, emphasizing "unity and coherence," teaching the research process, and thoroughly integrating bibliographic instruction into the broader curriculum, influenced instruction librarians in later years.[4]

No one was more influenced by Shores and Knapp, nor was anyone more influential in his turn, than Evan Farber, chief librarian at Earlham College in Indiana. Farber persuaded campus administrators to institute library instruction throughout the curriculum. The Earlham program emphasized "course-related" or "course-integrated" instruction. The instruction began in the required freshman humanities course and continued in subsequent, more specialized courses. With funding from the National Endowment for the Humanities and the Council on Library Resources, similar course-related programs sprang up at other undergraduate colleges throughout the 1970s. Prominent among them were initiatives at the University of Wisconsin at Parkside, Wabash College, Sangamon State University, and the University of Evansville. However, Miriam Dudley, college librarian at the University of California at Los Angeles, moved in a different direction with a self-paced library-skills program that used a workbook. Less labor-intensive than course-related instruction, it was more practical for large institutions with many students and was widely copied.

Most institutions named the service "bibliographic instruction," and it won rapid and wide acceptance in academic libraries. The success of bibliographic instruction during the 1960s and 1970s was due to its easy conformity to the public-service traditions of librarianship, the support it gave to academic librarians in their pursuit of professional status and enhanced prestige, the availability of resources for libraries during these financially favorable years, and the era's general dissatisfaction with the status quo, which generated broad educational experimentation. Eastern Michigan University librarians helped to institutionalize bibliographic instruction when they founded the Library Orientation-Instruction Exchange (LOEX) in the early 1970s. Also during this decade the ACRL issued "Guidelines for Bibliographic Instruction in Academic Libraries"; the American Library Association Council issued its "Policy Statement: Instruction in the Use of Libraries"; the *Journal of Academic Librarianship*, which includes a regular column on bibliographic instruction, came on the scene; and many professional library associations founded bibliographic-instruction roundtables or subdivisions. In 1983 *Research Strategies*, a journal devoted entirely to bibliographic instruction, began publication.

Changes in library instruction began to take place in the late 1980s. Concerns raised by rapid advances in information technology began to dominate much of the literature. The question of how best to prepare users to search online public-access catalogs and other online sources, as well as sources on CD-ROM, forced librarians to rethink what a reference source was, what the real challenges involved in seeking information were, whether there were qualitative differences between seeking information on paper and on a computer, and, if so, what they were, and what was the best way to develop students' information-technology skills. Increasingly, individualized hands-on instruction sessions took the place of sessions that emphasized lectures, slides, and audio-visual formats. Monitor screen projection and other computer-related technologies became increasingly important. In the 1980s, as in the 1960s, most of the writing on the subject assumed that library instruction was course or assignment related; however, the literature also reported that the instruction included library tours; credit courses in library skills; video, audiotape, or slide-show presentations; term-paper clinics; workshops or seminars geared to specific reference tools or subject areas; and handouts, handbooks, or point-of-use guides. The changes in thinking culminated in the information-literacy movement.

Information Literacy

Several documents on the ACRL website define information literacy. "Information Literacy Competency Standards for Higher Education," approved and published by ACRL on January 18, 2000, characterizes an information-literate person as one who can

> determine the extent of the information he or she needs; access the needed information effectively and efficiently; evaluate information and its sources critically; incorporate selected information into his or her knowledge base; use information effectively to accomplish a specific purpose; understand the economic, legal, and social issues surrounding the use of information; and access and use information ethically and legally.[5]

The Standards document emphasizes the importance of information literacy as a survival skill in today's environment of rapid technological change and proliferating information resources. It recognizes a range of areas where different kinds of information may be needed, including, but not limited to, academe, the work place, and personal life. The information may come from any number of sources, including libraries, community services, special interest organizations, the media, and the Internet. It may also be available in various formats, including graphics, sound recordings, and texts.

The Standards document goes on to describe information literacy as the basis for lifelong learning. This type of literacy is common to all disciplines, all learning environments, and all levels of education. It enables learners to "master content, extend their investigations, become more self-directed, and assume greater control over their own learning." The document also calls for a restructuring of the learning process that would abandon the teaching of facts found in workbooks, textbooks, or lecture notes and would instead embrace resource-based learning. It encourages librarians, faculty, and media and information-technology specialists to collaborate in their work to ensure that learners become information literate. The emphasis is on learning, not teaching, and librarians should play an important role in the learning process. Finally, information literacy, according to the Standards document, is related to the skills involved in information technology. The information-literate learner must know the technology and how to use it. However, information literacy has broader implications. While information technology focuses on an understanding of technology and the skilled use of technology, information literacy focuses on content, communication, analysis, information searching, and evaluation.

The New and the Old

There are in fact many similarities between the library-college and information-literacy movements. Information literacy's core ideas—that an information-literate person must be able to recognize an information need, locate relevant information, evaluate the information, use it effectively, and understand the economic, social, and legal issues relating to information—are ones that the American library profession has embraced for a long time. Louis Shores and other librarians involved in the library-college movement in the 1950s and 1960s wholeheartedly supported these core ideas, although undoubtedly the details and terminology they used in that support differed. They would have also agreed with present-day librarians that library instruction is common to all disciplines, all learning environments, and all levels of education. Also, both movements share the beliefs that learning is more important than teaching, that learning must be library oriented, and that independent study is a much better way to learn than classroom teaching. Shores saw the faculty person as a bibliographic counselor, and he thought librarians were especially suited for this counselor role. Information-literacy librarians are in complete agreement with this idea.

In addition, support for distance and lifelong learning is common to both movements. As World War II and Korean War veterans began returning to school in ever-increasing numbers beginning in the late 1940s and early 1950s, and as ever-increasing numbers of students enrolled in work-study programs and distance-learning courses, the student bodies of colleges and universities became less traditional and more diverse. Such factors as constant and accelerated change in the work environment and the need to be more mobile in the pursuit of better jobs coalesced to make distance and lifelong learning even more important. Finally, because of democratization and other social changes that took place during the decades following World War II, especially during the 1960s and early 1970s, new ways of teaching more diverse student bodies with different skill levels and using different information formats became very important. Shores saw these changes coming, and information-literacy librarians are still addressing the changes in their programs.

Information literacy emphasizes the importance of collaboration among faculty, librarians, campus staff, and other professionals much more so than advocates of the library-college did. Yet, Shores and his colleagues did support collaboration, especially between teaching faculty and librarians. Also, they understood that learners could get information from many media formats. They recognized that matching the individual differences of their students with the different media available was one of the most important services librarians and faculty should provide their students. Shores's concept of the generic book that included materials in print, audio-visual, and computer format is readily identifiable in ACRL documents on information literacy. These documents recognize the varied formats in which different kinds of information are found.

Both movements embrace the concept of universal and thorough instruction in library use. Information literacy calls for a restructuring of the learning process—a restructuring that would abandon the teaching of facts and instead embrace resource-based learning. Through this restructuring, learners would become more self-directed and assume control over their own learning. Shores likewise saw the need to revitalize or restructure library instruction as it existed then. He believed that instruction should cover use of the entire range of formats available to the learner. He also called for new ways to teach library instruction. Finally, to support what he hoped would become a nationwide effort, Shores wanted to see American higher education provide greater resources for library-instruction programs. Advocates of information literacy are looking for the same kind of support today, although, since funding from the private sector now plays a much larger role in higher education than it did in the 1960s, they often approach entities other than those the library-college advocates approached.

The revitalization of library instruction that Louis Shores and other advocates of the library-college called for has in fact been taking place. Since the 1960s, the library profession has increasingly embraced such concepts as independent, self-directed study, active, hands-on learning, distance learning, and lifelong learning. Many, if not all, library-college goals still live on as information-literacy goals. If there is a major difference between the library-college movement and information literacy, it is in the level of information technology. Today's learner must have a wide range of information technology skills. However, although these skills play an increasingly important role in library instruction, the tenets that govern instruction in the use of libraries and other related information sources have remained very much the same.

Both the library profession's efforts to address the rapid change in information technology, and the consistency in the philosophy and goals that have characterized first library instruction and then information literacy in recent decades, provide the librarian involved in information literacy a sense of adaptability and stability in this age of seemingly endless change. A time-honored past provides the stability. It gives substance and validity to information literacy.

Notes

1. Association of College and Research Libraries (ARCL), Presidential Committee on Information Literacy, Report by the Committee (January 14, 1989) recommendation no. 1, in *ACRL: Association of College and Research Libraries*, December 13, 2001, at www.ala.org/acrl/nili/ilit1st.html.

2. Melvil Dewey, "The Profession," *Library Journal* 1 (1876): 5–6.

3. Much of the information in this chapter relating to the library-college comes from *Encyclopedia of Library and Information Science*, s.v. "Library-College."

4. Much of the information in this chapter relating to bibliographic instruction comes from *World Encyclopedia of Library and Information Services*, 3rd ed., s.v. "Bibliographic Instruction."

5. Much of the information in this chapter relating to information literacy comes from Association of College and Research Libraries, "Task Force on Information Literacy Competency Standards for Higher Education" (January 18, 2000), in *ACRL: Association of College and Research Libraries*, January 5, 2002, at www.ala.org/acrl/ilcomstan.html.

He who learns, and makes no use of his learning, is a beast of burden with a load of books. Does the ass comprehend whether he carries on his back a library or a bundle of faggots?

—Moslih Eddin Saadi

CHAPTER TWELVE

Plexus and Nexus: From Ramelli to Zappa and Beyond

Fred Nesta

> . . . but if you want an education, go to the library.
>
> —Frank Zappa, 1967

Frank Zappa, one of America's more prescient philosophers, must certainly have perceived something about the future of libraries as early as the middle of the twentieth century—or what may have been the start of the current one. I attended an all-men's college, so I spent a lot of time in the library. I was self-taught, in that much of my education came from doing research assignments. At that time, there was no bibliographic instruction that I can recall. Benjamin Franklin had purchased the first books for the library; I may have even used some of them in my first paper—something on the French Revolution. I do remember that the library was old, the books older, and the green leather tabletops and Tiffany lamps made for a setting very conducive to sleeping while I studied John

Locke. In those days I never imagined that one day I would become a library director, but something from that time has stayed with me. Even today, I still insist that my library have a place where a student can read quietly, even though the rest of the library is a place for active discovery—a place where excitement fills the air, and the more mysterious and almost alchemical processes of education can occur.

Whether at the dawn of the age of the virtual library or centuries from now, whether in our world or on worlds yet to be imagined, libraries will always have a physical presence, not only as storehouses but also as places where education in the truest sense is fostered. A library is a place where a space in time and a quiet corner unite to allow thoughts to be transmitted, ideas to merge and emerge, and information to be absorbed and mastered. The physical structure of the library may change, as it has changed over the past twenty years, accommodating spaces for group study, computers, audio and video listening and viewing rooms, cafés and gift shops, children's rooms, conference rooms, and lecture halls.

In England I turned one of my libraries into an "open learning center," a place where students could meet with tutors or independently use library resources to learn language or mathematics skills—a sort of distance learning without the distance. Outside of academia, libraries are places where learning takes place, whether in public libraries where people study independently or in special or corporate libraries that provide a concentration of materials and a place away from a ringing telephone. Even with the proliferation of databases that bring information directly to a corporate researcher's desktop, there is still a place for the library and for the professional librarian as a researcher, organizer, and information provider.

Yet a library is more than a place. It is a point, a locus, a center—a nexus and a plexus. The physical structure of the library—its air-handling and book-handling systems—are important, of course, in providing a building to house our treasure-trove of precious books, documents, and media files, precious because of their irreplaceable intellectual and historic content; but today we can not limit the definition of a library to a place used for reading, study, or reference. What libraries have historically provided intellectually in one place, they now provide in their new role as a plexus, web, or network. That network can provide the nexus—a bond or link that connects things or parts. Frank Zappa also said, "Remember, in-formation is not knowledge; knowledge is not wisdom; wisdom is not truth." For those transformations to happen, a nexus, a bonding or link-age, has to occur that transforms information into knowledge and knowl-edge into wisdom.

I think the time is coming when every librarian will become less a part of the plexus of the library and more a part of the nexus that makes transformation possible. We may not quite live up to Spider Robinson's description of librarians as the secret masters of the universe, controlling all information. But in a world that former Citicorp chairman Walter Wriston said has "switched from the gold standard to the information standard," librarians are trained masters of information as central to the process of bringing order and understanding to the Information Age as our scribal ancestors were in preserving the heritages of the various clas-sical worlds that preceded us. While inaccurate, it has been claimed that the Internet is a like a huge library with books strewn on the floor and no catalog. In truth, the Internet is more like a comprehensive research library that collects all of humanity's varied output, from the classic and sublime to the most ephemeral, and makes it all "keyword searchable." It is a marvelous resource, but it needs skilled and concerned profes-sionals who can bring order and understanding to it, just as profession-als have with millions of other resources traditionally found in libraries and archives.

There are icons of Agostino Ramelli's book wheel and Vannevar Bush's Memex everywhere in the library I direct. Ramelli's engraving "Le Diverse et Artificiose Machine," published in Paris in 1588, shows a scholar seated in front of a large wheel that holds about a dozen books, all individually suspended on reading platforms. By spinning the wheel, the scholar could have quick access to any of the volumes. This is an early example of man's quest for easier access to information, and of the human desire to have facts or references quickly at hand. This same desire drove the construction of the first libraries—places set aside in temples where books of prayers and incantations and, later, other reference books were collected for the priests to use.

Bush had a vision similar to Ramelli's, but he compressed scholar's knowledge onto microfilm, making it accessible on the Memex (a com-bined desk and microfilm reader). It took mankind centuries to move from memorization to writing, from clay tablets to papyrus scrolls, from scroll to codex, and finally from codex to microfilm and telephone reference services. However, it took only a handful of years to move material from the early character-based, command-driven databases operated by specialist librarians to today's World Wide Web. Libraries exist to provide information to anyone who needs it, no matter where that person may be. It is because of this commitment that I am an unabashed "Internet librarian" and wholehearted advocate of "disintermediation," or giving the patron the skills, abilities, and tools needed to access information directly and immediately.

Some would say we are in an information revolution. I believe that what we are seeing today is not revolution, but evolution. Perhaps we are watching the culminating step as the air-breathing fish finally crawls onto dry land. Many of the reservations people express today about the lack of quality and absence of control of material on the Internet are little different from what our ancestors feared when Gutenberg invented a mechanism that allowed commercial establishments to print anything and distribute it to a mass audience. Was that a revolution? Perhaps, but as early as 300 B.C., Koheleth was already bemoaning the fact that "Of making many books there is no end" (Ecclesiastes 12:12).

The book, Archibald MacLeish said, is "an ingenious cipher by which the intellectual book is communicated from one mind to another." Technology may change, the number of readers and publishers may grow, but the end will always produce the same result: a joining of reader and text. To that end, there are two intermediaries: booksellers and librarians. Having been a bookseller, I am as distressed by seeing unread books in my library as I was by seeing unsold books in my bookshop. I am delighted when I see a reader find the book on the shelf that satisfies that reader's need for information, enlightenment, or entertainment, because that satisfaction justifies my work, personal judgment, and investment in putting that book on the shelf. If that need is satisfied by an electronic resource I have selected, purchased, or linked, and the reader comes to it from far away, in the middle of his or my night, so much the better; this is a new form of access free from time and space, even free from any expenditure on my part beyond the time taken to select and add it to my library. A library is not a merely a vault for books: a library preserves and protects but most of all makes things available to people.

While there is no revolution taking place in what libraries do in uniting books and readers, there is a revolution in what many librarians, particularly academic librarians, are becoming. Like Paladin's description of the knight chess piece in *Have Gun—Will Travel*, a librarian can be "the most versatile on the board. It [he/she] can move in eight different directions, over obstacles, and it's always unexpected." Today's librarians move in many directions and over many obstacles. The past few decades have forced an increase in the roles librarians play and skills they must have. We are no longer limited to the roles of curator and selector, but are increasingly becoming educators and publishers in our own right. The book is simple and straightforward in its design. Locating material in a book is a simple matter if it has an adequate index. Locating the book itself is equally simple if the library has a decent catalog—card or electronic. Except for certain idiosyncratic indexes, we never have to teach someone how to use a book. The new electronic resources are far more complicated and fluid. Their simple interface, which may be fine for someone looking for a "quick fact," but inadequate for a scholar, masks the underlying complexity. The people using these resources may be on the other side of the world, in their home library. Librarians not only have to teach their patrons to be aware of the complexities behind a search screen but also must find ways to reach remote patrons to provide them with access to data and assistance in using it.

Bibliographic instruction has now become information literacy, a skill recognized as critical by accrediting agencies. Librarians are delivering a literal world of information directly to patrons' desks, in far greater volume than Ramelli or Bush could have imagined, yet in a format that seems as simple as the original book wheel. We have an obligation to teach users that searching is far more complex than it looks, that databases are constructed and indexed in a manner unique to themselves, and that Boolean logic is operating behind the scenes in every search box. We must also teach them that search engines are different from databases and from Web directories and that each engine covers a different spectrum of the Web. And of course, we have to teach them that critical thinking applies to the Web just as much as it does to print. Just as anyone can hire a Web server, anyone can buy or rent a printing press or get the occasional spurious article accepted for publication by an academic review board. Even the most carefully peer-reviewed article may not escape valid criticism that may appear in the next issue of the quarterly. A critical, even skeptical mind is a requisite tool for any scholar, businessperson, or citizen.

A librarian as an educator is one part of a librarian as a nexus, as a transformer who guides users to the appropriate resource by teaching users proper techniques and making them aware of scholarly criticism. The other part of the nexus is a librarian as a creator and disseminator of knowledge who provides and preserves content. Librarians have always engaged in some internal publishing, preparing guides, pathfinders, and bibliographies. The Internet gives libraries an opportunity to go beyond such things. It allows us to publish not only our catalogs but also the content of the indexed books, documents, sounds, and images, making unique and important collections available to scholars worldwide. The American Memory Project at the Library of Congress, the Lester S. Levy Collection of Sheet Music at Johns Hopkins, the Electronic Text Center at the University of Virginia, the Gallica Classique collection of classic French literature at the Bibliothèque National, and the digitized Gutenberg Bible at the British Library are only a few examples. As digitization becomes simpler and less expensive, more libraries will be able to publish their important collections, whether the collections are important globally or only to their local communities. Publishing will also allow librarians to be involved in other fields, such as the promotion of items they publish and the development and implementation of new technologies.

Like traditional print publishers, libraries cannot afford to publish a collection of local historical documents and not let scholars or genealogists know of the collection's existence. Libraries must become promoters of themselves and their publications. They will have to develop new indexing tools to make it possible for readers to find new publications—some new union catalog of electronic resources.

It is libraries and librarians that will not only add to this new and complex web, this plexus, but as they act as educators, they will also be the nexus that will bring understanding and enlightenment to people everywhere. Then we can truly say to all those who desire to learn, "Go to the library and begin the transformation of information into your own knowledge, wisdom, and truth."

Upon this age, that never speaks it mind,
This furtive age, this age endowed with power
To wake the moon with footsteps, fit an oar
Into the rowlocks of the wind, and find
What swims before his prow, what swirls behind—
Upon this gifted age, in its dark hour,
Falls from the sky a meteoric shower
Of facts . . . they lie unquestioned, uncombined,

Wisdom enough to leech us of our ill
Is daily spun; but there exists no loom
To weave it into fabric; undefiled
Proceeds pure Science, and has her say; but still
Upon this world from the collective womb
Is spewed all day the red triumphant child.

"Sonnet," by Edna St. Vincent Millay

CHAPTER THIRTEEN

From Custodian to Navigator:
The Amazing Heroic Journey of
the New Information Specialist

William B. Badke

I really didn't realize the librarians were, you know, such a dangerous group. . . . They are subversive. You think they're just sitting at the desk, all quiet and everything. They're like plotting the revolution, man. I wouldn't mess with them.

—Michael Moore, Interview in *BuzzFlash*, March 13, 2002

Do you want to keep your job? A question like this seems so crass and self-serving that you might be tempted to ignore it. So let's phrase it in less visceral terms: do you want to ensure that the noble profession of academic librarian continues through this century and into the next?

You might feel the urge to answer my question with others: "Why wouldn't our noble profession continue? We, after all, are librarians. Librarians are forever. Where would the world be without us?"

Where, indeed? But did you know that there is an active conspiracy out there to remove us, to terminate us with extreme prejudice? Maybe the term "conspiracy" isn't entirely accurate, because the conspirators haven't discussed their plot much among themselves. Yet, they seem so in tune with one another that it certainly looks suspicious. So what is this movement that threatens to unseat our profession and put many of us on the unemployment line? It can be expressed in three words: "eliminate the mediator."

You see, technology has made it easy to believe that all information is accessible directly to the user. Picture your average undergraduate with four term papers to write. Did you know that this student, armed with a subscription to questia.com or access to ebrary or netLibrary, along with a password for your institution's online full-text databases or a remote subscription to XanEdu, not to mention the easy availability of google.com on the Internet, can write a pretty good research paper without ever entering a library, let alone making personal contact with a librarian? Students are library avoiders anyway. Now they have a way to make it work.

True, there's a whole lot more to libraries than a few databases and e-books. What about our rich collections of books and journals unavailable in any form except hard copy? What about the expertise of the librarian who can save the bacon of virtually any student and do it with panache? Surely we and our collections are still needed.

But are we? Let's face the cold truth here: 80 percent of the students we encounter are not genuine students at all. They're trainees in an academic program, doing the minimum required to get what they need and then leave academia for good. Spending time hanging around librarians isn't seen like a smart move on the way to a diploma. Even a significant percentage of the professors need us only when it's "publish or perish" time, and most of them never ask for our help. That leaves graduate students, who are likely our neediest population. But are there enough of them to guarantee that our profession will not be marginalized?

The bottom line is that mediators in our society are biting the dust faster than opponents of Billy the Kid. Think of all the stockbrokers no longer plying their occupations due to the many trades being made directly between investors and the stock market via the Internet. Think of travel agencies that are downsizing because potential customers can just as easily use the Net to book flights themselves (although anyone who has tried to plot a trip from Vancouver to North Carolina arriving at 4:30 P.M. knows the limitations of doing it yourself). People inherently like to avoid mediators, and now, with information so accessible, it's becoming easy to do so.

Charles Babcock has written about the phenomenon of the "Internet's Rust Belt," the place where technology tends to toss those who have become outmoded. He points out, "According to some economists, the Internet will one day replace anyone who enjoys a middleman position by virtue of the information he or she controls."[1] Why? Because mediators cost us time and money. Because going to a mediator involves an admission of personal inadequacy. Because we like to do things ourselves, and we resent others controlling our access to what we want. A recent survey of workers in knowledge-based industries showed that 68 percent of them preferred doing their own research, while only 3 percent consulted their institutional libraries.[2]

And so our profession is at risk because we academic librarians are mediators, and our patrons have found easier ways to get their information directly. Patrons never did warm to us, not really. (Just think of the mental image that the word "librarian" evokes.) Now they don't even need to acknowledge our existence unless they are forced to.

How did we get to the point where our very reason for being academic librarians is under attack? To understand our present and our potentially terrifying future, we need to take a brief trip through our history.

The Custodian

In the mid to late 1800s, when libraries in North America were first becoming forces to be reckoned with, the task of the academic librarian seemed clear—gather a first-rate collection of books and journals, catalog it, guard its safety, and provide reasonable access to it for authorized patrons. This role was little different from that of a modern manager of an auto parts store.

Yet even then in that simpler time, there were voices raised to elevate the role of library professionals from that of custodian of the warehouse to the loftier image of missionary or sales person or promoter and purveyor of intellectual wares. The fascinating article by Robert F. Nardini, "A Search for Meaning: American Library Metaphors, 1876–1926,"[3] points out the struggle among librarians of the era to add value to their role by seeing themselves as far more than keepers of the books.

Consider the following: Melvil Dewey in the premier issue of *American Library Journal* declared, "The time was when a library was very like a museum, and a librarian was a mouser in musty books. . . . The time is when a library is a school, and the librarian is in the highest sense a teacher.[4] Or this gem from John J. Thompson in 1897: "Books . . . have a mission, and the librarian and director who promote the circulation of books, become missionaries of the book."[5]

Of course, there were strict limits on how much value a librarian could add to the warehoused collection. In the earliest days, there was not even great reference service, because it was believed that classification numbers and subject headings were enough for most patrons. But librarians still made themselves indispensable. How? By limiting access to their collections. Wayne Wiegand reminds us of a paper presented in 1883 by Charles Ammi Cutter, entitled "The Buffalo Public Library in 1983." Cutter's vision of the library and those who would work there 100 years after his own time went like this:

> Individual reading rooms located nearest subject-classified stack collections were staffed by trained librarians with relevant expertise. And in the reading rooms he witnessed patrons working at desks equipped with "a little keyboard" wired to a central site that they could use to request a specific title from the closed stacks by punching in its classification number.[6]

In Cutter's view, the stacks would always be closed and helpful librarians would always be near to take requests and provide access to the books.

Even when reference service came on the scene, there remained a strong debate between the "point them in the right direction" and the "give them what they want" camps, with most reference librarians opting for the reference interview as an embarkation point for the patron's own voyage of discovery. In this way, the patron was left feeling foolish and numb, ever dependent on the custodian of the books, who seemed to be the only person who knew how to find anything with ease. Card catalogs, as most librarians are acutely aware, were never intended to be user-friendly because their primary users were to be librarians who knew what they were doing.

This secure and elitist role for the academic librarian continued right up into the 1970s. True, stacks were opened and reference service became more customer oriented, but the professionals still remained all-wise custodians, necessary mediators between patrons and the collections they knew so well. Academic librarians declared themselves to be important because no one had more skill at cataloging and referencing the contents of the warehouse than they did.

The Information Broker

The 1980s brought dramatic change to the librarian's role. These were heady times at first, because changes in academic library systems gave an unprecedented amount of control to the library professional. New periodical indexes emerged, government documents came into their own, retrospective conversion of library catalogs consumed immense numbers of professional labor hours. Then came the databases, electronically available from remote sites but too complicated and expensive to allow patrons to do the searches unaided.

Though times were changing, librarians were very much in control of the process, asserting their superior skills and knowledge in a way never seen before. Once again, however, this elevation of the profession came at the expense of accessibility for patrons. While anyone could walk into a university library, look up a subject heading, gather some books, consult a print index, pick up some journal articles, and leave the building unaided at any point, there was a sense during those days that things had become much too complicated for mere patrons to risk wandering around without help. Most universities had banks of subject-specialized reference desks that were a constant hum of activity. If you wanted to search one of those newfangled electronic databases, woe betide you if you hadn't booked an hour with your own personal library guide well in advance.

There was an all-pervasive feeling among librarians in the 1980s that patrons would never measure up, that they would always require help, much like a would-be traveler would always need someone to book his or her flight. Out of this grew a new model, that of the information broker. No longer could the academic librarian be a mere custodian. Patrons were needy, and with customer service a growing demand in academic institutions, our profession increasingly became the means to connect people with data.

The term "information broker" actually came from companies that did research in the corporate world for money, but the concept was a handy one for the library professional. In an era in which information was becoming an ever more useful commodity, and new digital resources were available from remote sites, it was a perfect time for librarians to position themselves as mediators between patrons wanting enlightenment and the sources of information themselves.

The Crisis

In one decade, the 1990s, we lost almost every watt of power we'd generated over 150 years. How did it happen? Why are patrons avoiding the library in increasing numbers and academic administrators wondering out loud whether that financial sinkhole known as the library is really worth the cash being spent?

Blame it on the fact that our importance as mediators faded for the same reason as the strategic roles of stockbrokers and travel agents are fading—patrons found new ways to get the information they needed all by themselves, often even bypassing libraries themselves. Direct access is the keynote of the new information age, but, as we have seen from our history, our power as librarians has consistently come from limiting access and putting ourselves forward as the only viable mediators for the informationally challenged.

The new age of the 1990s, however, delivered a fearful wound to our place in the information world. Consider the Internet, easily the most powerful force driving this phenomenon. It was built without librarians—attested to by the fact of the ludicrous choice to make the default on most search engines a Boolean "or." Most anyone can search the Internet without booking time with a librarian. Little children use it in their school projects. Senior citizens fifty years out of school plumb its depths, seeking gardening tips, recipes, and treatises on Confucian philosophy. What's more, it's a far more exciting environment than any library most people know and certainly more entertaining than any librarian could be.

Professors are telling me, and the library literature is full of confirmation, that student research-paper bibliographies abound with URLs, so much so that most professors have to set limits. Why would a student choose some inferior website as a research resource over a massive print volume published by Oxford University Press? Because it's easier—no middlemen, no library to struggle with. Students, being students, will prefer easy access over quality most every time.

Even textbook publishers are getting into the game. Beyond the now familiar book with CD in a pocket offering additional data and pictures to view at home, consider this recent gem from psychology texts published by Thompson Learning. Inside each book, there's a card insert with the caption, "Stop! Don't throw this away." It offers a four-month subscription to InfoTrac College Edition (also owned by Thompson). On the back of the card is the loaded comment: "*Time saver*—why travel to the library when you just need to look up a few articles?"[7]

So our gate counts are dwindling and our reference interviews are more about the proper use of electronic indexes than the proper subject headings for a study of Marie Antoinette. In fact, I sometimes imagine that if professors weren't forcing their students to use a variety of sources, we could sell all our print materials and open a huge computer lab. The hunger for electronic full text is frightening, and if you want a student to hate you as a reference librarian, all you need to do is pass on the news that the particular journal article wanted is only available on microfiche. I can't count how many patrons I've seen in such a predicament, who simply went back to the full-text index in search of something else that was electronic in format.

Even in the back rooms there is uneasiness. Those who once maintained vast periodical collections are under pressure to abandon hardcopy titles that are also accessible on ProQuest or EBSCO. More and more journals are publishing parallel versions online for a fee, while university administrators are canceling print subscriptions if these journals are deemed too expensive, regardless of whether or not there are cheaper alternatives of the same quality.

Catalogers are still managing catalogs, but book-collection budgets are under siege. With the growth of cataloging databases like OCLC, no wonder cataloging departments are shrinking in many institutions. Once again, there is less room for mediators between information and users.

Bob Ainsbury and Michelle Futornick, in an ironic twist, summed up the crisis in an article published in late 2000: "Twenty years ago, library scientists ruled the information retrieval world; they just didn't

know it. Now they are poised to return to the top of the far more lu-
crative Web world, and my hunch is they still don't know it."[8]

The irony? Their proposed solution is for librarians to abandon traditional librarianship in favor of showing their usefulness in the corporate
Internet arena. In effect, Ainsbury and Futornick are arguing that the
new information age has killed the future for the academic librarian.

The Navigator

H. L. Mencken believed that "There is always an easy solution to every
human problem—neat, plausible and wrong." What I have to say about
the new role of Navigator may certainly be said to fit that category, but
if I may coin my own quotation as an antidote to Mencken, "Insuffer-
ably paternalistic complexity is the enemy of problem solving." In fact,
paternalism is the reason why we put our discipline at risk of going the
way of the middle manager. We failed to see that we were keeping our
patrons needy and elevating our role by denying them free access.
Someone should have warned us that said patrons would eventually
make a bid for independence.

True, most university students still need us sometimes, and there is
probably some scope for a many of us to continue cataloging, signing
out books, answering reference questions, running systems, and so on,
for a very long time. But our patrons don't think they need us like they
used to. They don't want guidance through the research process.
They want us to show them how the databases work and then leave
them alone unless they ask for help. Even more seriously, there is a
sense out there that the barn door is wide open, and even more direct
access will come for everyone over the next few years. We haven't even
considered the potential impact of direct-to-the student online libraries like questia.com, ebrary, and XanEdu.[9]

It is my conviction that if we are going to hold our heads up high
and survive as librarians in the new information age, we are going to
have to take on the dangerous profession of navigator. To understand
this concept, we need to contrast it with the information broker of the
past. In the broker's world, there were patrons and there was information, and the task of the broker was to connect people with the information, wherever it might be. The broker was versatile and helpful,

now plucking a book off a shelf, then digging up a microfiche article or performing an online search. The broker had power because the patron was confused and lacked the ability to find what was needed in the increasingly complex world of the modern library. Yet, it is exactly that power that is now evaporating as our patrons increasingly learn how to use our systems themselves, often remotely from home.

Enter the navigator. The navigator knows that students can pilot their own ship and find their own way if they want to. But there are dangerous shoals and big rocks in the way that the navigator can negotiate more safely. In other words, while much of the voyage may be easy sailing, there is an assumption that there will come a time when every wise captain turns the wheel over to a navigator.

Simply put, we are speaking of an information specialist of whom it can be said that, no matter how fine your research may have seemed, this Navigator can help you do it better. But not by limiting access. Rather, the new academic librarian will simply have to be better at managing information than anyone else so that the strongest value-added component to whatever resources the library has will be the library professional. To the student, the navigator says, "I know you can find it, but I can find it better, and wisdom tells you that you'll need me sooner or later."

So how does a navigator operate in practice? Let me suggest three scenarios:

The Navigating Cataloger
Cataloging these days has entered strange territory. Now books come with CDs or even parallel websites with more graphics. We're entering URLs into records and turning our on-site OPACs into Web servers. What if, despite all the denials, printed books will soon be on the wane and electronic media will flourish to an extent previously unimagined? In such an environment, the cataloger who's also a Navigator will shine.

The first time I heard that people were actually trying to catalog the Internet, it seemed as ludicrous to me as trying to empty the Atlantic with a thimble. But I'm not laughing anymore, because librarians all over the world are recognizing that cataloging the Internet is the work of a navigator. True, anyone can search the Net, get 2,457,923 results, and maybe find that two of them are relevant. But the Internet can't tell the user which sites are of better quality, more accurate, easier to use, and so on. As D. M. Sendall puts it, "We need to organise a social cyberspace more like the real world, where we can tell the difference between a reference library and a nightclub."[10]

Bringing order to cyberspace is the work of a cataloging navigator who can use specific criteria to locate and create records of the sites that are going to be the most productive for the student. Certainly, this might be seen as a type of censorship but no more so than what is done in the average acquisitions department. What the navigator adds to the Internet is the use of selection criteria and the provision of a broader arsenal of search tools such as controlled-vocabulary subject headings. Anyone can search the Net, but the navigator provides the means to do so much more effectively and certainly more discerningly.[11]

Beyond cataloging the Internet, librarians are hard at work providing catalogs for the numerous full-text periodical resources now available and enhancing monograph records with relevant Web addresses. Whatever is done to add value to the ordinary patron's electronic research is as much the work of the navigator as is creating a record for a print edition of *The Iliad*.

Information Literacy

Give a man a fish and you feed him for a day; teach him how to fish and you feed him for a lifetime. This is the sentiment behind the information-literacy instruction done at most universities—empower the student to know where to find information and what to do with it, and that student will be a researcher for life.

At first glance, this may seem to be a nail in the coffin of the library professional. If we teach our students how to do research, they won't need us anymore because we've empowered them with the tools that make direct access workable. In fact, the very opposite is the case, as I've observed consistently during my sixteen years of information-literacy teaching. You see, students don't know how much they don't know until they have an opportunity to learn more. The average student knows how to access the Internet, search a library catalog, and do some basic work on EBSCO or ProQuest; thus, there is great resistance to research training. But that training, once given, opens up a new world. Students are amazed at what's possible when research is done well. Once they get some training and become self-navigators, they tend to deepen the level of their research, thus finding new opportunities to ask for help from the professional navigator.

Far from making the librarian irrelevant, information literacy humbles the freshman know-it-all and elevates the student's perception of library professionals, who really understand how systems work. I find that information literacy generates more reference questions rather than fewer, but they are better questions than, "How do I get onto this EBSCO thing?" When librarians are seen as those who can unveil what's possible, navigators come into high demand because students have broken through the mediocrity of easy direct access and found a world where information is valued and those who can make it more accessible are treasured.

Reference

Most reference librarians know that they have to perform or die. It's a dangerous world out there on the information desk, more akin to a hospital emergency ward than the lonely booth from which Lucy in the Peanuts cartoons dispensed advice. True, many of the questions asked have to do with the operation and repair of databases, but the average professional on the reference desk (unless a specialist) is as likely to be asked for a book that has photos of pond larvae as for a website that provides the full text of a treatise by Aristotle.

To be a navigator in such an environment is to do a lot more than point patrons in the general direction of what they need or to broker the connection between student and relevant data. To be a navigator is to be, in a carefully calculated way, amazing. Students should regularly be able to look at us with wonder and ask, "How did you do that?" Our reputation should spread all over the campus as the people who can help you find stuff when all other efforts have failed. True, students will continue to lust after direct access without mediators, but a well-positioned reference navigator can persuade them that independent research is fine only until you see the need to bring someone on board who knows where the obstacles are.

How do reference librarians become amazing? They do it by being better than anyone else at handling information, no matter what its format. I believe most of us are there now, but we need to market ourselves as never before. Don't leave students satisfied; leave them stunned. When you see someone looking confused, approach that student and declare that, whatever the problem, you can help. When you've helped in a search, do some fast thinking about what else you could bring into the situation that would flabbergast the student with its relevance. Kick yourself every time you fail to find what was asked for and then do enough research on your own so it doesn't happen again.

Some librarians are not up to the challenge. They feel they should be respected and valued without having to scramble. These are the ones who will go the way of the dodo bird, because, face it, we're only as good as the last question we answered. Tomorrow's reference librarian will look more harried, and may feel like the target at a Robin Hood archery contest, but, by gum, the successful information professional will be a navigator, valued because students know that a good librarian is pure gold.

One more battlefront faces all navigators—the tendency in our patrons to favor direct access over the pursuit of quality. Here is where librarians and professors will have to conspire together to stop rewarding mediocrity with good grades. All types of navigators will have to work to make quality a valuable commodity—the cataloger who provides even better access to good materials than most ill-conceived search engines ever could; the information-literacy specialist who opens up new worlds of knowledge accessibility; and the reference librarian who proves the claim, "whatever you can find, I can find better."

New models of positioning ourselves within the library are emerging, the most exciting being the "information commons," where a maze of computers and databases are married to a strong social atmosphere and where navigators not only provide access to worlds yet unknown, but circulate among the searching patrons, helping them steer clear of the big rocks and find safe harbor. Food, drink, and conversation are being encouraged, and no one stands in the way of free access. Users know that they are not alone, because the navigators are there.[12]

Academic librarians are still the best people for the job, but the key to our survival is selling ourselves to our waiting patrons. In coming days, when someone who hasn't seen you in action asks you who you are, pull yourself up straight and say boldly, "I am a navigator!"

Notes

1. Charles Babcock, "Do You Live In The Internet's Rust Belt?" *Interactive Week* September 17, 2000 9:00 PM PT.,September 6, 2001, http://www.zdnet.com/zdnn/stories/news/0,4586,2624946,00.html.

2. Kathy Dempsey, "Does your Manager Know?" *Computers in Libraries*, 21 (September 2001): 6.

3. Robert F. Nardini, "A Search for Meaning: American Library Metaphors, 1876–1926," *Library Quarterly*, 71 (April 2001): 111-131.

4. Nardini, "Search for Meaning," 112.

5. Nardini, "Search for Meaning," 118.

6. Wayne Wiegand, "This Month, 116 Years Ago," *American Libraries*, 31 (January 2000): 104.

7. Insert in 2001 psychology textbooks published by Thompson Learning.

8. Bob Ainsbury and Michelle Futornick, "The Revenge of the Library Scientist." *Online* 24 (November/December 2000): 60.

9. For a discussion of the potential impact of questia, see my article, "Questia.com: Implications of the New McLibrary," *Internet Reference Services Quarterly* 5(3) (2001): 61-71.

10. D. M. Sendall, "The Future of the World Wide Web and Its Impact On Our Institutions," in *The Impact of Electronic Publishing on the Academic Community*, London: Portland Press, 199), October 2, 2001, http://tiepac.portlandpress.com/books/online/tiepac/session1/ch6.htm.

11. Examples of such catalogues of the Internet include Library HQ's Site Source, http://www.sitesource.com/; MERLOT, Multimedia Educational Resource for Learning and Online Teaching, http://www.merlot.org/Home.po; and OCLC's CORC project, Cooperative Online Resource Catalog, http://www.oclc.org/corc/.

12. See Donald Beagle, "Conceptualizing an Information Commons," *Journal of Academic Librarianship*, 25 (March 1999): 82-89; Tim Lougheed, "Libraries Gain Clout and Cachet In the Information Age," *University Affairs* (October 2001): 9-11, 17.

70 percent of all archaeological research is done in the library.

—**Professor "Indiana" Jones**

CHAPTER FOURTEEN

Giving Away the Keys to the Kingdom

Rebecca S. Graves

You cannot teach a man anything. You can only help him find it within himself.

—Galileo

Some librarians fear that by teaching others how to search for information, we assist in the ending of our profession. Once the "end user" learns how to find information without us, we will be sent off to the closet that holds buggy whips and passenger trains. Are we causing our own demise? Is it possible that all of what we know can be condensed into a one- or two-hour course? Is this all that is of value from what we have learned in the various masters programs we attended and our years on the job?

On the other hand, while we may fear that we will undo ourselves by giving away the keys to our kingdom, are these keys even wanted?

Are the students and faculty willing to listen? Are they seeking our knowledge? Perhaps they want to open locks that our keys do not fit.

Fear has many faces. Perhaps the worst is obsolescence. To no longer be valued may be a fate worse than no longer having a job. Most of us will be able to get another job; however, we entered the library profession because we valued it. To think that we could, that we might, become obsolete, is more than lost pay; it is a loss of heart.

Can We Give Our Jobs Away?

If my job consists merely of showing people which box to check on the screen, how to use Boolean logic, and how to use "Internet math," then yes, I can be replaced by Web tutorials, manuals, or cheaper nonprofessional instructors. These are rules that are readily learned—formulas or recipes that can be memorized or read. They are, in most cases, the foundation for knowledge of a subject. For example, I can purchase a book on German grammar and learn it without a teacher. If I am a musician, I can memorize the circle of fifths. True, it is often faster to have another person show me the teachable tasks; however, the point remains that it is not necessary. I do not need an instructor to teach me these rules; I can learn them on my own.

If this is so, then what is my role as an instructor? My role is to learn what they cannot teach themselves. While I can teach myself the grammar and even the vocabulary of a language, I cannot teach myself the subtleties of a language. When, for instance, would a German speaker use the word "doch"? Which idioms are used and when? What facial expressions and body language are allowed or not allowed? These are all things that can't be taught. To be fluent in a language, I must have the opportunity to use it; and I must have feedback. This is what a teacher provides—the chance to use information, to experience it, to roll it around in the mind. Ideally, the teacher creates the space, need, and safety that the student requires to learn. As George Allen writes, "Teachers are for . . . helping students learn what they can't be taught."[1]

What do librarians know that can't be taught? Several skills come to mind: organization of information, critical evaluation of sources, filtering, extrapolating, synthesis, and the research process. I can teach you pieces or theories of all of these; however, without experiencing them, you will not learn them. Specifically, I can give you rules to use in evaluating a source; you can memorize these basic rules, yet not learn them. To have learned something means to have the ability to apply it, which takes thought, experience, and feedback. A student can go automatically down the list of evaluation criteria—author's credentials, scope, reviews, and so forth—yet not learn much. Learning a rule and learning how to apply it are two very different skills.

Most of what I teach falls under comfort. Comfort is the ability to perform a task without being "flooded." The student may need to think consciously about what she is doing and may do it haltingly; however, she is not overwhelmed with anxiety. In my "one shot" library-instruction sessions, my goal is to make the students aware that specific resources are available to help them with their particular courses and that these resources are accessible both on and off campus. My hope is that this will allow the students to be comfortable enough to ask questions when they actually start in on their projects and papers. That is, by having a face for the library and having heard the names of databases and other terms, students will feel less threatened by the library, more comfortable asking for assistance, and less anxious about using the databases.

My next goal in the same session is to teach the students the theory and rules for using these resources and to teach them the steps they need to take to access them, whether on campus or off. By this I mean rules and procedures that are usually easily memorized or learned by rote, such as the library Web address, the name of the subject database to use, and the commands for executing a subject search. This piece is taught with the hope that—through practice and critique—the students will eventually become competent in the use of these various resources.

Competence—composed of knowledge, skills, and attitude—is the ability to perform a task efficiently and well. It is the ability to function highly at known tasks and in known situations. Competence is the ease and ability of one who has proven confidence in, as well as comfort in with, her skills. Having learned a language, the competent speaker can use it fluently to clearly express his ideas and thoughts. Having learned the scales in the circle of fifths, a competent musician can apply them in her performance. Similarly, with research, I know the resources and rules of how to use them, and I am able to apply those rules to carry out the process.

This cannot be learned through a book or Web page. To reach this level, I need feedback about my actions. If I use a certain phrase, do people understand me? Do they raise their eyebrows in puzzlement? When doing research, I get feedback in the answers and information I find. However, I learn more when I get feedback from a human teacher as to the efficacy and efficiency of my search, the appropriateness of the database that I have chosen to search, and the focus of my topic.

That I would have time in one class to reach the third goal of having the students learn how to apply this knowledge and develop mastery is beyond idealistic—it is impossible. One session does not even provide enough time to finish goal two of teaching the students what they need to know to develop competence, not to mention creating the space in which the students can learn mastery.

The test of mastery is the ability to use knowledge and skills in an unfamiliar context, the ability to improve my performance. I know that I am masterful when I can adapt what I know—what I am competent at—to a new task or situation. I am a masterful speaker when I can use my foreign language to converse on topics unknown to me and to understand jokes or various accents. One who is a master is not thrown by change. Rather, she is uses her competencies in order to grow.

Both comfort and, to an extent, competency are "teachable." The information covered—for instance, who the librarians are, the names and subjects of databases, the pathway for off-campus access—can be learned from text, either in print or electronic form. It is not necessary to have another human present to learn these facts, rules, and procedures.

It could be argued, however, that competency does not fall neatly into either information that is "teachable" or information that is "learnable." Rather, it has elements of both. For example, knowing how to manipulate the search interface from a particular vendor actually involves at least two skills: first, knowing the rules that can be learned from the manual; second, knowing how to apply the rules. This requires "learning," meaning experience in using the interface. Not all experiences are equal. Experience that is won through failure and success, with thought put into both, is superior to experience gained by simply going through the motions.

Mastery is "learnable," but not "teachable." To become a master requires not only time but also testing of skills or knowledge in new and unfamiliar situations. Along with this comes the requirement to regularly evaluate performance through feedback and reflection.

Learning Space

Helping the students learn what cannot be taught requires the creation of a learning space. Space encompasses more than the room or lab in which the workshop is conducted. Space in this sense includes the outline and the boundaries of the topic at hand, the ground rules of the classroom, and thought and reflection.[2] Space is the place, both mental and physical, where students and instructors enter to learn and teach.

Within this space there must be safety. The old-school method of teaching through ridicule and fear leaves students better able to cover their ignorance than to ask questions and to seek out learning. To get beyond comfort and reach mastery, students must feel safe to ask stupid or roughly phrased questions. They need the space in which to make mistakes without ridicule.

Creating safety requires ground rules that prohibit destructive criticism on the part of the students as well as the instructor. It also requires that the instructor refrain from cynicism and sarcasm. A safe space requires that the instructor actively encourage questions verbally and also by having the students write them out beforehand. Encouraging mistakes and using them as learning opportunities also makes the classroom safe for learning.

As important as safety is need. Why is the student here? What is the purpose of the assignment—to get a grade, pass a test, get a degree? Much has been made of "point-of-need" or "just-in-time" learning. When possible, this is the ideal. Yet not everything can be learned in this way. Surgeons need to know how to perform a surgery before they step into the operating room. Travelers need to know at least a few words of the language before they can communicate. The need must be created. Ultimately, the student must motivate herself; however, the teacher sets the path with assignments relevant to the topic at hand and intimations of how these skills will serve the student in her larger life. How to do this is currently being explored in the areas of active learning, problem-based learning, and information literacy.

All of this may appear Herculean, and it is indeed a challenge. I may not succeed as well as I like, yet I continue to try. For if I fail to help students and faculty to learn, then I surely am risking my job.

And this is not all. I must also demonstrate to others the difference between what can be taught and what needs to be learned, between comfort and competence in the finding and use of information.

Your Silence Will Not Save You

I must open my mouth and be heard. I must illuminate, perhaps even create, the need for librarians to become instructors, and then I must speak. In a strict sense, I must speak of teaching as instructing someone how to find information. However, I must broaden this to include teaching about what I do.

Demonstrations of library resources and services to outside departments and one-on-one orientations or teaching sessions can be used to sell library services. After all, when given a thirty-minute slot for orientation on a day when the students are flooded with information, the best approach might be that of an infomercial. With no assignments yet, no hands-on training, and a mind full of questions about where to go, it is unrealistic to expect students to remember, much less care about, the fine points of accessing and searching subject databases. Better to leave them with a positive feeling that the library is their library and offers them crucial services that can be accessed simply by calling 555-BOOK or typing www.library.edu.

I must spend less time selling the hammer and more selling the skills of the carpenter. In addition to extolling the resources that the library offers, I need to be selling my own abilities at acquisition, searching, fact finding, and education. For example, when complimented on the work I have done, it would be better for me to say, "I'm glad you noticed," rather than, "Oh, it was nothing." Instead of thinking of this as "blowing my own horn," I need to think of it as spreading the word that the library is more than a list of databases and the undergraduate student at the circulation desk.

Marketing versus Promoting

It strikes me that just as much of library instruction aims at comfort, many of my attempts at marketing aim at promotion. In this case, I refer to marketing as the aggregate and promotion as a subset. To paraphrase Philip Kotler,[3] marketing is the collective task of determining the needs, wants, and interests of our users and then delivering their desires better than the competition. Promotion, on the other hand, is publicity, advertising, and disseminating information about the library's services. Clearly, promotion is just one of the many tasks that falls under marketing. Promotion practiced alone is often blind and inefficient. Like broadcasting seeds, I hope that the message is meaningful and gets to the right people at the right time; and just like broadcast seeds, the message is just as often wasted, falling where it won't grow.

Marketing is global and therefore allows more strategy. Before expending time, energy, and money on promotion, I first need to gather information on my customers. Who are they? What do they want? What do they need? Who are my competitors? And I need to keep gathering information. It does not stop with one survey or focus group.

Another task that falls under marketing is strategic planning— charting a course for where the organization wants or needs to go. Such planning provides a centerboard, keeping the library from being blown off course from its goals. After all of this come promotion and publicity.

While many librarians know this well, few libraries have the staff and time to run a comprehensive marketing plan. Adding strategy sessions, creating and analyzing user surveys, and completing the other assorted task of marketing may seem an impossible burden. Yet, it is a strategy that libraries and librarians must adopt. Have I asked our users what they want, need, expect? How can I keep my job if I don't know my audience? Setting time every five or seven years for reviewing the library's values and strategy is better than never. No time for a formal questionnaire mailed to my whole user population? I can set up a quick and dirty poll on my Web page. The point is that I cannot afford to let the excuse of perfection keep me from using the tool of marketing. If I am able to find the time and money to produce posters, bookmarks, exhibits, and workshops, surely I have some time and money to strategize which posters, exhibits, and workshops will be the most profitable.

We are aiming and hitting short of the mark whenever we downplay the understanding needed to find and use information well. We can aim higher by openly acknowledging our skills, strategizing the future courses of our respective libraries, and educating others as to our value. While information is more easily accessed now than in the past, it is not necessarily easier to find the appropriate information. Our users may or may not be aware of their need for assistance. In either case, it is our job to educate them about their information needs and to persuade them that we are the ones qualified to assist them.

We only give away the keys to our kingdom if we let them drop—if we fail to pay attention to what our users want and need, and if we do not teach what we have to offer. By telling others what we do and showing them how we support them, we are ensuring not only that we will keep the kingdom but that we will continue to have a market for the keys as well.

Notes

1. George Allen, "The Art of Learning with Difficulty," in *Future Teaching Roles for Academic Librarians* (Binghamton, N.Y.: Hawthorne Press, 2000).

2. Parker J. Palmer, *The Courage to Teach* (San Francisco: Jossey-Bass, 1998).

3. Philpp Kotler, *Marketing Management: Analysis, Planning, Implementation and Control*, 8th ed. (Englewood Cliffs, N.J.: Prentice Hall, 1994).

What one has not experienced, one will never understand in print.

—Isadora Duncan

CHAPTER FIFTEEN

Shining Some Light on the Monster under the Bed: A Closer Look at the "Doubling of Knowledge"

Martin Raish

> One of the diseases of this age is the multiplicity of books; they doth so overcharge the world that it is not able to digest the abundance of idle matter that is every day hatched and brought forth into the world.
>
> —Barnabe Rich, c. 1613

We have all heard the mantra: knowledge is doubling every [insert your favorite number] years/months/days/hours, and so on. Knowledge is a monster of hideous proportion.

Or is it?

The "knowledge is doubling" specter in its various guises has haunted us for generations, as illustrated by the Barnabe Rich quotation, but it gained increased attention with the rise of the Internet and the development of personal computers in the early 1980s. Today, many people, including librarians, seem to be frightened by this beast, judging by the hundreds of times it is mentioned in books, articles, speeches, news reports, and websites. A tiny sample (a half-dozen years' worth) of such statements follows. I could have included many other examples (my most recent Google search for "knowledge is doubling" returned over 600 hits), but these will suffice. They are arranged chronologically:[1]

- 1995a "Our worldwide knowledge fund doubles every six to seven years."
- 1995b "Knowledge is doubling every 16–18 months."
- 1995c "We are in a period when knowledge is doubling every 16.7 months."
- 1995d "Knowledge is doubling every three hundred and fifty days according to those who calculate such things."
- 1996a "At the current rate, the entire body of scientific knowledge will double every two years."
- 1996b "Knowledge is doubling every 3–5 years."
- 1996c "It is estimated that the amount of medical knowledge doubles every two years."
- 1997a "The total of all printed information doubles every five years."
- 1997b "The reservoir of world knowledge is doubling every two years."
- 1997c "Human knowledge is doubling every thirty or so years."
- 1998a "Human knowledge is doubling every ten years."
- 1998b "The store of human knowledge is doubling every five years."
- 1999a "Scientific and technological knowledge doubles every three to five years."
- 1999b "In 25 years, knowledge will double every three months."
- 1999c "Knowledge is doubling every six months."
- 1999d "Recorded knowledge is doubling every 15–20 years."
- 2000a "All printed knowledge doubles every five years."
- 2000b "The total of all printed knowledge doubles every four or five years."
- 2001a "Advances in technology and technique now double the total information astronomers gather annually."

- 2001b "The amount of available knowledge is doubling every 18 months."

I have long had serious reservations about statements such as these. Let me explain why.

Data, Information, Knowledge

My first concern is simply the lack of precision about what exactly is growing. While most of the statements speak of "knowledge," I discovered the majority of them while searching for "information." They were taken from speeches and articles about "The Age of Information" or "the information explosion," yet they cite how rapidly "knowledge" is growing. Information and knowledge, however, are not the same thing. (Nor is either the same as data, another term people sometimes confuse with them.) We need to understand clearly the distinctions among these terms.

Pieces of data are things lying about. They can be natural phenomena—the temperature of the air, the size of a seed, the weight of a lion, the composition of the soil, and so forth; or they can be man-made—prices of goods, sports scores, dimensions of buildings, and so forth. There seems to be no end to data.

Information is more than data. (As Clifford Stoll in his book *Silicon Snake Oil* has observed, "Data isn't information any more than fifty tons of cement is a skyscraper.") It has been defined in many ways, but two of my favorite definitions are "facts without context and therefore without priority,"[2] and "the meaning that someone assigns to data."[3] The critical aspect is that for information to exist, a person must gather and ponder data and arrive at some decision that usually results in an action being taken or at least a choice being made. This action or choice may be immediate, or the information may be filed away for future use.

And just as information is built from data, so is knowledge built from information. Knowledge is information that has been internalized, that has become "mine" and is different from "yours." It is what results when I gather and ponder information, evaluate various conflicting ideas and experiences, then apply it to my circumstances to make it part of my life. It is also something that rarely results from anything other than sustained effort or direct experience. Thus, it generally has longer "staying power." It is more permanent, less open to the winds of change.

Knowledge is also difficult to communicate. When you try to share with me what you "know," it comes to me not as knowledge but as information or perhaps even as data, if there is distance between us either in time or in the number of intermediaries who have translated, reworded, or summarized the ideas along the way. I must recreate my own knowledge with the information I have received. Thus, the term "printed information" (1997a) is acceptable, but "printed knowledge" (2000a, 2000b), "recorded knowledge" (1999d), or even "available knowledge" (2001b) are more difficult for me to accept.

One way to illustrate the differences in these concepts is to picture yourself driving in your car toward a railroad crossing on Main Street in your town. The tracks are data: they are just there. The times of departures and arrivals are also data.

Information is formed when you see the tracks, read the timetable, and recognize it as the correct one for your location. You then combine this with data such as the day of the week, the time of day, and the fact that you plan to be in town several times this week.

Knowledge is the realization not only that the train arrives at 12:05 on Tuesday afternoon but also that the day is Tuesday, the time is 12:04, and you are approaching the crossing. All the data and information you have gathered and considered now combine to become valuable to you. (Wisdom, of course, is to stop your car and wait for the train to pass.)

All this is probably moot, however. The people who made the doubling statements likely never thought about my concern. For them the terms are almost certainly interchangeable.

I have no doubt that the amount of data is growing at an astounding pace, as we discover more about our natural world and create mountains of "artificial data" in our man-made world. If these statements spoke of "data" instead of "knowledge" or "information," I would have a much smaller quarrel with them. The fact that they do not discriminate between the terms is a serious weakness they all share.

Measuring or Guessing?

My second reservation with these statements is their significant disagreement as to exactly how rapidly information/knowledge is growing.

The differences cannot be explained because of the years in which the words were written, as if the pace of growth were accelerating. The two quotes about "scientific knowledge" (1996a and 1999a) illustrate this problem: it is doubling every two years in 1996 but every three to five years in 1999. It is also important to note that the extremes are separated by only two years: we have thirty years' doubling time in 1997 but only six months doubling time in 1999 (1997c and 1999c).

Similarly, for the same year (1995), different statements have this doubling occurring within years, months, and even days. Either we are not all using the same instrument to measure growth, or the tool we are using is inaccurate. It is also possible that we are not using any measuring instrument at all but only making educated guesses, based on limited observations of data that is sketchy at best.

Furthermore, in order to claim that something is growing, we must not only measure it now but must have also measured it sometime in the past using the same (imprecise) tool. Has this been done? Yes, but rarely, since there are few situations where accurate measurements are even possible. One is to count the number of publications in a particular field and calculate how rapidly it increases. For example, we can determine how long it took Chemical Abstracts to index its first millionth entry, its second millionth, and so forth. Because fewer years elapsed between each milestone, it is reasonable to conclude that the number of publications in the field of chemistry is growing. But the data simply does not support the contention that any sort of doubling is occurring very quickly.

If we define "doubling" as the total number of items cited since Chemical Abstracts began keeping track, the data shows that the most recent doubling took about seventeen years, from 9,904,000 items in 1983 to 19,754,000 in 2000. If we define "doubling" as the number of citations listed each year, the data shows an even longer period: in 2000 there were 725,195 citations, but we must go back to 1975 to find a figure about half this size.[4] Thus, the data reveals periods of seventeen or twenty-five years, not two or three or five, as these "experts" claim. (A similar analysis of Biological Abstracts showed that the literature of biology increased by about 80 percent between 1984 and 1994—a faster pace than that of chemistry but still far from doubling in just a few years.[5])

Even if we acknowledge that the pace of scientific publication is accelerating, can we conclude that all knowledge is growing at a similar rate? Such an extrapolation, I believe, is unjustifiable.

Documentation

The third factor that erodes the value of these statements is that the authors provide no documentation for their claims. One statement does mention "those who calculate such things," and others (not cited here) occasionally make passing reference to the number of articles or books published in a year, or some similar bit of data that could be verified (or not). But every time I have tried to uncover the source of a growth number, I have run into a dead end.

For example, a scholar was quoted in a national publication as saying that "the amount of electronic information is doubling every 60 minutes."[6] I contacted him and asked for his documentation. I learned that what he was really talking about was the number of electronic records generated everyday, including short-lived banking and business transactions, and satellite downloads of weather and military surveillance data that are not really "information." He had gotten his figures from a colleague, who in turn had read them in a report,[7] the methodology of which was described as being "at best, back of envelope."

What originally appeared to be a rare case of a well-documented study of the growth of information proved to be a mirage. (I should also note that the source where I first found the statement neglected to mention that it was a prediction, that the growth was not happening today, but was expected to occur "within ten years.")

It is undoubtedly true that data is being discovered and generated at a fantastic pace and that the amount of information we deal with daily is prodigious, but none of the statements about the "doubling of knowledge" have enough real evidence to persuade me that it is increasing at anywhere near the rate many people are claiming.

Information and the *New York Times*

There is one other assertion that appears at least as often as those that speak of the "doubling of knowledge." I like to think of it as "the mother of all information growth quotes" because it has been around for more than a decade and has been repeated ad nauseum: a weekday edition of the *New York Times* contains more information than the average person was likely to come across in a lifetime in seventeenth-century England.

This is usually attributed (if at all) to Richard Saul Wurman's book *Information Anxiety*.[8] And while it has been quoted dozens of times, many writers apparently could not resist the temptation to "improve" it, as illustrated by the following variations:[9]

- Every issue of the *New York Times* contains more content than a seventeenth-century individual would have read in a lifetime.
- A single daily edition of the *New York Times* contains more information than the average seventeenth-century person needed to know in an entire lifetime.
- On an average workday, the *New York Times* contains more information than any contemporary of Shakespeare's would have acquired in a lifetime.
- One Sunday edition of the *New York Times* contains more factual information than all the written material available to a reader in the fifteenth century.
- One copy of the Sunday *New York Times* contains more information than most educated men and women 600 years ago read during their entire lifetimes.
- If you were to read the entire Sunday *New York Times*, you would absorb more information than was absorbed in a life time by the average American living in Jefferson's day.
- Just one edition of the Sunday *New York Times* contains more information than our great-grandparents had to process in their entire lifetimes.
- The daily edition of the *New York Times* contains more information than your grandfather encountered in a ten-year period.
- The front page of the *New York Times* contains more information than an entire half-hour news program.

While I have doubts about the value of these statements that are no less worrisome than those I outlined for the "knowledge is doubling" group, they at least do not suffer from a confusion of terms: all but one use the word "information." (The exception speaks of "content.") However, like the earlier statements, these reveal a total lack of concern for validity, since none of them presents even a shred of documentation to support its claims. (Not even Wurman cites his source.)

Furthermore, I suspect that one of these quotes (the fourth) is false. By the end of the fifteenth century (only fifty years after Gutenberg's first efforts), there were tens of thousands of books in Europe. It is difficult to believe that even a year's worth of Sunday newspapers could equal their combined amount of information. (It is also interesting to note that this source cited several other "facts" to support the author's description of today's information glut and provided footnotes to all of them except this particular one.)

What fascinates me most about these statements (and others like them not included here) is the variety of words they use to describe the ways people interact with information. People

- Read
- Acquire
- Absorb
- Encounter
- Process
- Need to know
- Gather
- Are exposed to
- Come across
- Receive
- Learn
- Accumulate
- See

Are these all the same activity? Do people necessarily absorb everything they encounter? Do they need to know everything they are exposed to? Or receive? Or see? Does it matter if a person reads, or processes, or gathers? Is to "come across" the same as to "accumulate," or is to "learn" the same as to "acquire"? I do not think so. The differences among these activities are as important to grasp as those among data, information, and knowledge. They are not interchangeable words.

Reading information from the newspaper today—not studying, not even trying to remember it—is vastly different from the process of gaining knowledge practiced by people in earlier times (whether 600 or only 200 years ago). They truly needed to know to survive; today we likely read more for entertainment.

Furthermore, a huge proportion of a modern newspaper does not contain "news." What value would advertisements have for peasants in seventeenth-century England? Did they need to know baseball box scores? Stock prices? Claiming that they "came across" fewer such "news" items really has no meaning. On the other hand, does the newspaper report crop planting instructions or tell us how to help a cow give birth to a calf?

Our ancestors absorbed/learned/gathered not by reading (which many of them could not do), but by observing nature, talking with peers, and asking questions of elders. Our ancestors' needs, resources, and information-gathering processes were all different from today's.

I am not persuaded that the sentiment of either Wurman's original statement or any of its variations is worth much. Any comparison of a modern newspaper to the information needs of the past should be for-ever banned from use by information professionals.

If we need additional incentive to support such an interdict, it might be found in the fact that all these statements rest on a weak foundation. The earliest account I have found that compares a modern newspaper to an ancient knowledge base comes from a speech given by the Eng-lish politician Richard Cobden: "I believe it has been said that one copy of the *Times* contains more useful information than the whole of the historical works of Thucydides." His address was given in Man-chester on December 27, 1850.[10]

Is it possible that Wurman and all the others have been basing their statements about today's newspaper on what was believed in 1850? Since none of these people provide any documentation, we may never know.

This review of statements about the growth of information/knowledge has revealed a fundamental confusion about what is being measured, a crucial inability to measure whatever this might be, and a total disregard for seeking documentation instead of repeating unsubstantiated rumors, especially apparent in the case of uncritical dependence on a 150-year-old anecdote. Together, these factors lead me to conclude that the "Knowledge Is Doubling" monster is, to a large extent, more a mirage than a reality. Some sort of creature is lurking under the bed, and it is probably large, but it is not so huge that we should be paralyzed by its mere shadow. Shining a flashlight on it reveals its lack of substance and shrinks it to a manageable size.

Notes

1. The sources for the following statements were found via searches conducted using Lexis-Nexis or Google, and complete documentation (especially page number) is sometimes unavailable:

1995a Robert P. Bevan, "System, Not Teachers, at Fault," editorial in *The Arizona Republic* (26 February 1995). [Accessed via Lexis-Nexis.]

1995b Albert Warson, "Dr. Tomorrow Is in Today," *Forbes* (December 4, 1995): 20.

1995c Jamie H. Jenkins, "Acceptance Speech," National Association of County Agricultural Agents (August 1995).

1995d William C. Merwin, "Taking off the Blinders and Squint a Bit to See What Might Be," New Student Convocation, State University of New York at Potsdam, August 24, 1995.

1996a Bill Felkey, "References for Rapid Recall," *American Druggist* (June 1996): 37.

1996b Ralph Marston, "Keeping Up with the Pace," *The Daily Motivator* (27 March 1996), January 10, 2002, at www.greatday.com/motivate/960327.html.

1996c M. O. Hotvedt and M. J. Scotti, "Continuing Medical Education: Actually Learning Rather Than Simply Listening" [Letter], *JAMA* 275(21):1637–39.

1997a Wilson da Silva, "Information Overload May Be Killing You," *The Professional Reading Guide for Educational Administrators* 18(2) (February/March 1997): 1.

1997b Terry Hilliard, "Improve Your Reading Techniques," *New Straits Times* [Malaysia] (2 December 1997). [Accessed via Lexis-Nexis.]

1997c Rudolf Hanka, "Information Overload and 'Just-in-Time' Knowledge," *Proceedings of the 4th Hong Kong (AsiaPacific) Medical Informatics Conference 97*, June 19, 2002, at www.medinfo.cam.ac.uk/miu/papers/hanka/mic97/just_in_time.html.

1998a Attributed to Michio Kaku by Melvyn Bragg, "Time to Get Fit for Being Homo Superior," *The Times* (March 16, 1998). [Accessed via Lexis-Nexis.]

1998b Bill Clinton, "Two Views of the Future of Science" [editorial], *Journal of Commerce* (March 26, 1998). [Accessed via Lexis-Nexis.]

1999a Attributed to Charles Vest [President of M.I.T.], *The Daily Yomiuri* [Tokyo] (January 25, 1999). [Accessed via Lexis-Nexis.]

1999b Attributed to Douglas Englebart. *San Jose Mercury News* (September 15, 1999).

1999c "Merits of Educational Technology," Mountain Brook City Schools' Technology Plan [Mountain Brook, Alabama], June 19, 2002, at www. mtnbrook.k12.al.us/techno/techplan/merits.htm.

1999d Donna Berg, "How Are Scientists Using Journals?" LANL [Los Alamos National Laboratory] Research Library Newsletter (January 1999), June 19, 2002, at lib-www.lanl.gov/libinfo/news/1999/9901.htm.

2000a S. Hadi Abdullah, "Have We Lost the Art of Thinking?" *New Straits Times* [Malaysia] (20 July 2000). [Accessed via Lexis-Nexis.]

2000b Jack Trout, *Differentiate or Die: Survival in Our Era of Killer Competition* (New York: John Wiley, 2000), 74.

2001a Attributed to Paul Messina, *Newsbytes* [*Washington Post*], October 30, 2001, at www.newsbytes.com/news/01/171661.html.

2000b *Bayer Group Webzine*, September 12, 2001, at www.bayer.com/en/webzine/makrolon/

2. Wendell Berry, "Thoughts in the Presence of Fear," *Orion Online*, October 30, 2001, at www.orionsociety.org/pages/oo/sidebars/America/Berry.html.

3. Peter J. Denning, "When IT Becomes a Profession," in *The Invisible Future* (New York: McGraw-Hill, 2002), 298. He adds, "Information thus exists in the eyes of the beholder; the same data can be nonsense to one person and gold to another."

4. CAS Statistical Summary 1907–2000, February 2001, at www.cas.org/EO/casstats.pdf.

5. Bernadette Freedman, "Growth and Change in the World's Biological Literature As Reflected in BIOSIS Publications," *Publishing Research Quarterly* 11(3) (Fall 1995): 61–79.

6. John L. King quoted in *American Libraries* (August 2000): 34.

7. Rich Lysakowski and Zahava Leibowitz, "Looming Information Age Crisis Expected to Cause Trillion-Dollar Losses over Next 20 Years," CENSA [Collaborative Electronic Notebook Systems Association], 2000, June 19, 2002, at www.censa.org/html/Press-Releases/Titanic2020.htm.

8. Richard Saul Wurman, *Information Anxiety* (New York: Doubleday, 1989), 32.

9. The sources of these statements are as follows:
   a. Gerry McGovern, "Egovernment: Epublisher, How the Web Is Changing the Way Governments Communicate with Their Citizens," NUA Ltd., March 2, 2001, at www.nua.ie/nkb/egovernment/chapter3.shtml.
   b. M. Thaxter Dickey, "A Brief Description of the Postmodern Condition," 1998, at theanimist.netgazer.net.au/pg000034.html.

c. Attributed to John Sealy Brown by Jon Desenberg, "Moving Past the Information Age: Getting Started with Knowledge Management," *Information Impacts*, July 2000, at www.cisp.org/imp/july_2000/07_00desenberg.htm.

d. Thomas H. Davenport and John C. Beck, *The Attention Economy: Understanding the New Currency of Business* (Cambridge: Harvard Business School Press, 2001), 4.

e. www.bergercollection.com/html/welcome/intros/thechallenge.html [Link has gone dark].

f. Wm. van Dusen Wishard, "The American Future: A Perspective for Education," a speech delivered at the Center for Educational Leadership, Lansing, Michigan, June 19, 1992. Available in *Vital Speeches of the Day*, vol. LIX, no. 1 (October 15, 1992), 20.

g. *The Littlestown Chapel Compass* 1(8) (February 26–March 4, 2001), at littlestownchapel.org/compass/v01/08-20010226/allweek.html.

h. Attributed [without acknowledging the changes] to Richard Saul Wurman in "cd-r/rw white paper" by the Verbatim Corp., 2001, at www.verbatim.com/products/products.cfm?sub_id=25&sub_lnk_id=27.

i. Mr. LaSpina's home page, Bethpage High School, Nassau County, New York, at www.bethpage.ws/~llaspina/aboutme.htm.

10. Columbia World of Quotations, via Bartleby.com, at www.bartleby.com/66/25/12725.html.

Andy Rooney points out that the Sunday edition of *The New York Times* has more information than he knows what to do with.

—Promotional blurb for Rooney's
60 Minutes commentary

The average person reads 150 words a minute, so if you read for eight hours a day, it would take you 14 days to read the Sunday edition of *The New York Times*, by which time, of course, you'd have two more in the driveway.

—Andy Rooney, December 9, 2001

CHAPTER SIXTEEN

Libraries As Gardens: Using Analogies to Teach the Research Process

Monica Ollendorff

Make books your companions; let your bookshelves be your gardens: bask in their beauty, gather their fruit, pluck their roses, take their spices and myrrh. And when your soul be weary, change from garden to garden, and from prospect to prospect.

—Ibn Tibbon (Spanish Jewish scholar, c. 1120–1190?)

Do you find yourself thinking more and more often of your instruction classes as groups of unruly monsters that need to be tamed before they assault your library? Do you have very few positive feelings about students who only want to know which button to push? Are you tired of thinking of new ways to present library-instruction material and have it accepted, understood, and taken to heart by your students?

Using analogies that are easy for your students to relate to may be the answer—not just to explain some of the access tools but to teach the entire research process.

Library instruction used to be easy. All we had to cover was the card catalog and a print index or two. Now it involves an online catalog, print indexes, electronic databases, keywords, evaluation, search strategies, Boolean logic, e-periodicals, ever-changing terminology, and the World Wide Web. The importance of teaching the research process to provide the basic structure for using all these new access tools has never been greater, and it's never been more difficult.

Using analogies that are familiar to students greatly enhances the learning of new concepts and facts. Freud said, "Analogies decide nothing, that is true, but they can make one feel more at home."[1] Naomi R. Sutherland and C. M. Winters wrote:

> Actively seeking connections between real life and information retrieval concepts will not only keep students' interest but also will also improve their ability to recall key principles when faced with the next research assignment. . . . One of the few recurring concepts that appeared in the literature is that analogies possess a power to create similarities between otherwise difficult-to-understand material and something that the student already understands or finds easy to understand.[2]

Diane Halpern, Carol Hansen, and David Reifer explained, "Analogies are useful instructional tools because they make abstract concepts concrete and therefore easier to remember, and they facilitate the exchange of ideas by providing a common terminology and framework."[3]

The use of analogies is part of concept-based instruction. In bibliographic instruction, they can help students learn principles and concepts, rather than just specific tools. As students learn how to use the library effectively and efficiently, they must learn librarian terminology and research techniques. Analogies familiar to students can bring this important information home. Creating analogies requires effort, and teachers must be comfortable using them; but they offer a creative, fun way to think about how to present the information they teach.

There are numerous analogies for individual items or individual parts of the research process. The following were contributed as part of a discussion on the bibliographic-instruction listserv (BI-L) online forum.[4]

Search Techniques

"These are like weapons in the searcher's arsenal—key words are precise, like shooting a sniper's rifle. Subject searching is like a machine gun that blankets the whole area." (Thomas Mann)

Indexes and Indexing

"Grocery stores use different methods for organizing products. For example, coffee pot filters may be near paper products, or coffee, or small appliances. This is the same way that different indexes organize information." (Robert Sinn)

"An index is like the Yellow Pages." (Barbara Greil)

Continuing this idea, if you want to send flowers to your mother and look under "Flowers," you are directed to "Florists"; "T-Shirts" are found under "T-shirts," but "Automobiles" has subheadings for buying, renting, repairing, body shops, restoration, and washing.

Database Selection

"The menu board at McDonald's indexes items by type of food. McDonald's could also index by prices, fat content, and size. But the main board only lists what is available at McDonald's. If you want a bucket of fried chicken, you must go to KFC." (John Riddle)

"Database selection is like going to a shopping mall. You can find almost anything at a general department store [InfoTrac]. CINAHL and PsychLit are like specialized boutiques." (Christine Guyonneau)

Call Numbers and Citations

"These are like license numbers and car registration. They both need specific information." (Sue Critchell)

Electronic Indexes

"Using a new database is like borrowing a friend's car. You know it has headlights, but how do you find where to turn them on?" (Kathryn Johnston)

"Learning to use electronic indexes is like learning to ride a bicycle. The first few trips are done just to learn how, and you wobble around and might fall off a lot. When you learn to adjust, you start trying to go places." (Marcia Keyser)

Database Searching

"A simple search is like trawling with a net when you go fishing. It takes little preparation. You get a big catch and 'trash fish.' In library speak, that is high recall, no precision. A more refined search with Boolean operators is like fly-fishing. Fly-fishing requires more forethought but the catch is smaller." (Moira Smith)

Online Catalog

"Learning to use an OPAC is like learning a video game. Becoming comfortable with the nuances of the program takes a lot of trial and error." (John Riddle)

The Research Process

"Learning this process is like learning a computer program. First, you may be tentative and unsure of the best ways to use the program. But software companies produce manuals and 800 phone numbers to help. In the same way, libraries [have] live human beings at the reference desk. It is normal to feel unsure about the research they are doing at first, but it will get better." (Barbara W. Petruzzelli)

"If you want to make a chocolate cake, you don't just go to the first store aisle and grab the first five items there. Instead, you carefully choose the ingredients needed for the recipe you have selected; you evaluate the several brands of different ingredients and choose the best. Then you can follow the recipe and end up with a what you wanted— a good chocolate cake." (Martin Raish)

"When you want to take a driving vacation, you select a destination, decide on your wardrobe, buy any clothes or other items you need, have the car tuned-up and the oil changed, plan the route and estimate how long the trip will take, based on the road maps you gather. While you are on your way you might need to evaluate road and weather conditions and accommodate detours as you progress, changing your plans or getting additional information as necessary, in order to arrive at your destination." (Martin Raish and Monica Ollendorff)

The selection of which analogies to use involves several considerations, such as who is in your audience, your geographic location, and how much actual demonstration you would be comfortable with doing in the classroom. One analogy that seems to work with almost any group is food. If you are teaching a class of college freshmen, fast-food analogies might work well, although health foods such as nutrition bars or salads are also popular among students. In some regions of the United States, salsa would be welcome; in others, greens would be more acceptable.

If you'd like to use salad making as a metaphor, would you be at ease bringing some lettuce and tomatoes, cucumbers and green peppers, a bowl, and a knife to class to demonstrate selection, evaluation, and balance to get a nice-looking, pleasant-tasting whole? Would you bring in a couple of bottles of salad dressing to point out that without a common bond, each ingredient isn't really an integrated part of a whole? Maybe using an oversized bowl for very few ingredients, or one that is too small for all the stuff you have to put in it, is more your style. On the other hand, if you can't stand brussels sprouts or eggplant, don't use them for analogies!

Inspired by the quote from Ibn Tibbon, I set out to develop a detailed analogy for the research process and all of its components. This is what evolved.

An important foundation is to understand that just as there are many different types of gardens, there are also many types of libraries. A vegetable garden is used primarily for food production, whereas a flower garden is intended for decoration and beauty. An herb garden has features of both. A small family garden is much different from a formal public one. And within any garden, individual plants are chosen for their capability to contribute to the overall impression the gardener deems desirable. Not every vegetable garden has green beans or every flower garden roses.

In a similar manner, libraries collect resources depending on the needs of the populations they serve. Students wishing to do research in a public library may be discouraged because of its emphasis on adult fiction and children's story books, rather than on scholarly journals. Even using their own academic library can lead to disappointment, since it has been shaped by the demands of the various programs it serves. If the university has no medical school, then the selection of medical journals will be limited. On the other hand if the theater department is one of the largest on campus, then the size and quality of materials for its majors will be impressive. Cacti won't grow everywhere, but you can be overrun with zucchini.

A library is a garden where a person is free to browse, explore, get to know some sections in detail, and pluck items for whatever need is at hand. Yet while simply browsing through a garden or a library may be a pleasant activity, and some unique or hidden treasures can be discovered, it is not the best way to choose flowers for an arrangement, select veggies for a meal, or to do research. Haphazard searching and too much dependence on chance can result in a disorganized bouquet of incongruous flowers or vegetables or a disorganized collection of incongruous bits of information for a research project. The way to avoid these disappointments is to follow the research process.

The scholarly research process is an organized method of seeking information on a subject. The first step is to state the idea, concept, or topic in the student's own words. The initial research statement should be broad, identifying the general direction in which the researcher is interested in going. Finding the right plants or seeds for an herb garden, a rose garden, a cutting flower garden, or a vegetable garden will require different strategies and resources. It also helps to decide whether the goal is a five-minute speech or a fifteen-page paper. Is the plan to sell produce at a roadside stand, design a floral centerpiece, or add an interesting blend of herbs or spices to an existing recipe? Having answered questions such as these, it is then possible to begin looking for background information by doing some basic fact finding in the reference collection of the library.

Even a small library will have general and subject-specific dictionaries, encyclopedias, directories, bibliographies, handbooks, atlases, and statistical sources. Using the reference collection can provide brief discussions or lists of definitions or facts that can bring the initial search statement into focus. Are there names, dates, places, events, or statistics relevant to the subject? The reference collection can also help clarify some points: How long has this issue been discussed? Is there a significant person or event that impacted the issue? Is data available to indicate progress or effect over a period of time? Are there terms that must be used in any discussion of the topic? Are there alternate terms that will lead to information? The student can use these pieces of information to refine his or her initial idea into a clear statement or question. Thinking about our garden again, is there a new hybrid available?

What will grow in which climate or which type of soil? Are there botanists or master gardeners whose advice ought to be followed?

If a student cannot find a subject-specific encyclopedia on her topic right away, she shouldn't dismiss the library as a whole. Just because her favorite rose is not in the first section of the rose garden she visits, that doesn't mean that there isn't anything pretty to see in the entire garden or that she won't find her favorite in the third section.

Identifying the types of information sources to use is the next step. The question to ask at this point is whether the student can expect to find information in books, periodicals, government documents, the World Wide Web, or other resources. In most cases, the answer will be that a variety of materials is appropriate. Books can provide in-depth information covering what has been evaluated or reviewed over the time period in question. Scholarly journals will provide researched commentary and reports, while magazines and newspapers will provide more popular points of view and public opinion. Searching the World Wide Web can provide a wide variety of information, from scholarly to popular. Should I buy seeds or live plants from a catalog or the local nursery? Should I read a book or two on the type(s) of plants or veggies I'm interested in? Do I need *Better Homes & Gardens* articles or articles from a professional agriculture journal? Should I sign up for the newsletter from the local horticulture society or go to their meetings?

This procedure is like deciding which flowers will make the prettiest bouquet or which will last the longest after they are cut based on color, size of bloom, height of stem, and so forth. Are leafy green vegetables more appropriate for the meal than corn or beans? The complementary processes of narrowing the topic while working through various resource materials are necessary before final decisions can be made.

Subject and keyword searches in the library's online catalog identify materials available in the library and where to locate them. The shelves provide the items identified in the catalog. Browsing the rest of the shelf where the identified item is found will turn up other items on the same topic. Indexes and databases, in print and online, identify magazine, journal, and newspaper articles on the topic. If one's passion is for berries, find the largest berry patch to see the most varieties. Sometimes this takes work, and students should be reminded to watch out for thorns when reaching for blackberries!

After finding and reading the articles, additional accents can be considered to add spice, color, and flavor to the already collected materials. These might be speeches or interviews found by exploring items identified in the reference lists of the books and articles retrieved, like discovering a lovely flower while walking down a side path in a garden.

Students sometimes find items that they don't like at first glance, such as spinach or broccoli (peer-reviewed journal articles or statistical tables). But with further examination and a trial taste, students should begin to appreciate their value. There are a variety of types of materials in a library for a reason. Including the odd jack-in-the-pulpit, fern, or hybrid rose on a regular basis is great for a research paper or speech. Students may not like them, but they need to understand their nutritional and research values.

Having gone to shelves in the library and picked out flowers and greens with their varying colors and scents, as well as some herbs and spices, and perhaps having peeked in some previously unexplored areas of the library/garden (special collections? government documents?), the researcher must evaluate the materials and organize them into a pleasing final arrangement. He must decide which point(s) of view to include in the final report, what order to put them in, how one section flows into another, which will predominate, and even which pieces of the gathered information might have to be discarded as not fitting in. The quality, accuracy, and reliability of the authors and the materials must be considered, as must their relevance and capability to combine into a unified whole. How do the colors, size, length, and texture of the flowers that were picked go together best? How is the flower arrangement to be displayed? Should the bright orange day lily make a striking focal point or does it just not fit in, in spite of how pretty it is?

Libraries are like large community garden plots, with different sections and departments being planned, seeded, cared for, weeded, and occasionally rearranged to make a valuable, interesting, and easily accessible whole. There are expected items such as encyclopedias and a few more exotic ones like special collections. Using the research process, the student can approach the library and what it holds, select one item here, two there, and perhaps include a spicy accent or two in the paper or speech.

While I do not plan to bring gardening tools and potting soil to class, or to ask the students to bring in flowers to arrange, or to put pots with different types of plants or hanging bunches of drying herbs throughout the library collections, I will say that creating this analogy for the research process has made the research process all the more real to me. The cohesion and rhythm of moving through its steps seem to flow even better in my mind.

I groom my houseplants regularly, along with repotting them, moving them around, and taking cuttings. I have now begun to apply that same process to my library-instruction practices, and I encourage you to do the same.

Notes

1. Sigmund Freud, *New Introductory Lectures on Psychoanalysis* (New York: W.W. Norton, 1933).

2. Naomi R. Sutherland and C. M. Winters, "The A, B, Z's of Bibliographic Instruction: Using Real Life Analogies to Foster Understanding," *The Reference Librarian* 73 (2001): 293–308.

3. Diane Halpern, Carol Hansen, and David Reifer, "Analogies As an Aid to Understanding and Memory," *Journal of Educational Psychology* 82(2) (1990): 298–305.

4. A summary was prepared by Jeanette Murrell and posted February 27, 1966. It can be found in the BI-L archives at bubl.ac.uk/mail/bild/9602.txt. The name following each idea is that of the person who contributed it.

If you have a garden and a library, you have everything.

—Cicero

CHAPTER SEVENTEEN

On Specialization

Kerry Smith

> Knowledge is indivisible. When people grow wise in one direc-
> tion, they are sure to make it easier for themselves to grow wise in
> other directions as well. On the other hand, when they split up
> knowledge, concentrate on their own field, and scorn and ignore
> other fields, they grow less wise—even in their own field.
>
> —Isaac Asimov

Almost gone, it seems, are the days of the Renaissance man, the universal scholar, even the well-grounded and well-rounded humanities
professor. The deluge of information, raw and processed, and the accompanying exponential growth of knowledge are naturally occurring
elements in the advancement of any civilization. The concomitant evolution of academia has resulted in specializations with intense and narrow foci, magnifying minuscule segments of learning to such an extent

that their concentrated investigations produce enormous amounts of understanding and prodigious publication records, mysterious and meaningless—some would say useless—to those outside their concentrated spheres. Universities teem with professorial positions in microfields of extraordinary emphasis and seemingly arbitrary designation—Middle Eastern feminist sexual philosophy, 1500 to 1503, or sub-Saharan Judaic labor-relations film studies—demonstrating the drift from parent discipline to proliferating sub-sub-sub-disciplines. Ultraspecialization is becoming the rule, not the exception, leading to serious repercussions, with liberal education, expansive scholarship, and diverse professional skills at the top of the casualty list.

Academe in ancient Greece and Rome consisted mostly of mathematics, music, and gymnastics, but Aristotle's eventual emphasis on the natural sciences added new branches of learning. During the Middle Ages, the emergence of monastic schools and universities facilitated the further division of knowledge into seven liberal arts: the *trivium* of grammar, logic, and rhetoric, and the *quadrivium* of arithmetic, geometry, astronomy, and music. From the Renaissance to the present, knowledge has undergone a slow but progressive mitosis, accelerated by the information explosion of recent decades. Without some kind of recourse, the effective management of enormous amounts of information—and its successful and meaningful transmission via the academic ideal of a universal, liberal education—could not help but be mired in the unceasing onslaught of knowledge. The natural recourse was, and remains, specialization.

From Immanuel Kant's model of the mind—an intellect equipped to understand the world only insofar as the world is processed by the mind's innate classificatory structures—one could speculate that a certain amount of specialization, via categorization, is helpful, necessary, and perhaps unavoidable. The organization, study, transmission, and reception of knowledge in discrete units aids in systematic exploration and discovery. But there must be a point at which a sliver of knowledge becomes so atomized as to be worthless to anyone but those few who study and understand it in great detail.

This danger applies equally to all areas of academe. Librarianship in large college and university settings has become such an extremely specialized occupation that a serials librarian often may not understand what a reference librarian does all day, or an archivist's work may be an utter mystery to an instruction librarian. When these well-trained, but narrowly experienced, individuals eventually rise to library directorships, they may be incapable of visualizing in a meaningful, comprehensive manner the complex interaction of their library's vastly disparate components. Effective administration will be hobbled by the inability to fully understand the daily functions and duties of many librarians or even of entire departments. The best—and perhaps only—solution to this problem is for administrators to spend time acquainting (or reacquainting) themselves with all departments and all functions of their libraries. They should walk the floors, work an hour or two at the reference desk, catalog a few monographs and serials, process some interlibrary loans, shelf read, file microfiche, place book orders. In short, they should remain current, connected, and at least semicompetent in a variety of library skills.

The specialization problem certainly transcends management, however. The academic library, a dynamic, polymorphous organism, mimics a significant organic quality: holism. Reference, special collections, cataloging, circulation, serials, government documents, acquisitions— these and all departments and professionals depend on each other for equilibrium and high performance. When professionals specialize to such a degree that they cannot understand each other's roles, duties, or even terminologies, the effectiveness of the whole is diminished. Academic librarians are typically more susceptible to the impairments of specialization than are public, school, or special librarians, who normally are proficient at most or all library functions; for libraries with few staff members, there is simply no other choice. Conversely, many contemporary academic libraries, due to their size and scope, are solidly supported by comparatively large complements of specialists. But a blessing can also be a curse: along with a staff of specialists come unique problems that academic libraries must address if they are to be healthy and effective organizations, serving their users fully and satisfactorily.

The trouble begins in library-science programs. Many programs do not provide rigorous, or even thorough, training in the variety of library tasks that graduates may be assigned to do when they begin their first job. Perhaps worse, library programs may recommend or even require that their students specialize in areas of librarianship. By actively limiting students in this way, programs inadvertently downgrade skills, undermining professional range and initial marketability. To correct this problem, programs should encourage a generalist approach, arranging curricula so that students master the full variety of library skills through practical courses. Courses emphasizing theory without relation to practical application should be reassessed. And programs should provide an abundance of extensive internship opportunities at the end of the coursework, or a series of brief opportunities throughout the coursework that mirror the curriculum, compelling students to employ all the tools of librarianship learned during their programs.

But vocational preparation should not end with graduation. It is incumbent on libraries to take active roles in their new employees' professional development. Librarians freshly graduated from library school and newly hired to their posts must be adequately prepared for and experienced with the entirety of librarianship, in whatever direction the profession may take them. Once in a specialized position for a length of time, a librarian's mobility may be restricted to two options: advancement within the organization (which could be limited, and in any case expedites the metamorphosis into the deficient administrator discussed earlier) or lateral movement to similar jobs at other organizations. To remedy this, the new librarian's first several months should be spent learning and doing the basics of every department in the library through orientation, observation, training, and applied experience. It is crucial that the conceptual wall between public and technical services be broken down during this period, providing all librarians with valuable exposure to the interlocking variety of roles; failure to combine all these vital roles into a cohesive intellectual whole—the entire library as the service—can lead to insular and territorial thinking, a severe detriment to vision and creativity. Furthermore, supervisors should encourage their charges to participate in seminars, conferences, workshops, and online discussions in areas outside of their specialization—and supervisors ought to attend as well, living the classic leadership maxim that managers should be willing to perform the tasks expected of their subordinates. Of course, if participation is expected, the administration should show its support through fee reimbursement and travel funding whenever the budget will permit it.

But new librarians are not the only ones at risk for multitask incompetence. Librarians who have been practicing—presumably as specialists—for months, years, or decades also need attention. The modern academic library is something of a Tower of Babel, filled with specialists speaking disparate languages. Those unacquainted with functions or tasks outside their immediate sphere cripple the overall effectiveness of the entire organization through uninformed decision making, vague planning, uncreative resource allocation, un-realized personnel potential, and uninspired individual and depart-mental collaboration. In addition, a library system composed of intensely specialized individuals, lacking the benefit of cross training, will respond to internal turmoil slowly and with inflexibility, if not paralysis. Illness, promotion, retirement, resignation, reorganization—these and similar events can cause chaos in an organization populated with specialists. A library staff composed of longtime, entrenched spe-cialists also risks the development of territorialism. The mindset is understandable: investing all of one's energy and time for years in a single duty or department invariably results in a kind of soft-toe syn-drome, manifested in turf wars, noncollaboration, noncreativity, information hoarding, and developmental rigidity. Quite simply, terri-torialism left unchecked can debilitate a library. But it can be over-come: a reduction in specialization should produce a reduction in territorialism. Crippled effectiveness, pandemonium, and territorial-ism can be averted through methods mentioned earlier, as well as through job shadowing, refresher training, and continuing educational opportunities (especially if a library school stands nearby), local host-ing of workshops and seminars, and encouragement to read widely in the professional literature (and a larger investment in subscriptions if the local professional collection is weak).

Regrettably, the adverse effects of intense specialization do not reach only librarians; the ripples reverberate throughout every facet of the organization. Academic library patrons are at risk of poor ser-vice from a specialized environment. When a profession that exists to serve is hampered from within, service is the first area affected. Li-brarians questioned on matters outside their immediate specialty can do little but shuttle the asker from department to department, in-creasing frustration with each transfer. Faculty with unusually com-plicated document-delivery needs find that their requests cannot be fulfilled because the specialist is on vacation. The online catalog crashes, but the systems librarian is at a conference, and no one else has received training for the solution. A student is desperate to locate complex chemical data, but the science librarian is at lunch. The circumstances are universal, but the solution is simple: despecialization.

But what is to be gained from despecialization? For those inclined to cost-benefit analyses, the library becomes more user-friendly, more efficient, and more economical in every way, achieving a higher return on personnel investment. But there are also benefits that cannot be quantified. Librarians develop greater confidence in their abilities as their skills broaden and deepen, initiating a corresponding improvement in morale. Individual and organizational flexibility increases. Territorialism decreases. Those academic librarians who are expected to publish generate substantial scholarly research in the field as a product of wider experience and deeper knowledge. The profession is enhanced, the practitioners are enriched, and the library is fortified.

Academic librarianship is a liberal art, as well as a science. The profession as a whole does not function well and cannot develop far as an intensely specialized pursuit. It cannot deny itself its rich, multifaceted, holistic past. It must not permit itself to be sorted, classified, categorized, and diluted to the point of collapse. In *The Stones of Venice*, John Ruskin wrote, "It is not, truly speaking, the labour that is divided; but the men: divided into mere segments of men—broken into small fragments and crumbs of life, so that all the little piece of intelligence that is left in a man is not enough to make a pin, or a nail, but exhausts itself in making the point of a pin or the head of a nail." We should work to ensure that academic librarianship stands as an exception to Ruskin's observation.

The archdeacon gazed at the gigantic edifice [of Notre Dame] for some time in silence, then extending his right hand, with a sigh, towards the printed book which lay open on the table, and his left towards Notre-Dame, and turning a sad glance from the book to the church,— "Alas," he said, "this will kill that."

Coictier, who had eagerly approached the book, could not repress an exclamation. "Hé, but now, what is there so formidable in this: 'GLOSSA IN EPISTOLAS D. PAULI, ~Norimbergoe, Antonius Koburger~, 1474.' This is not new. 'Tis a book of Pierre Lombard, the Master of Sentences. Is it because it is printed?"

"You have said it," replied Claude, who seemed absorbed in a profound meditation, and stood resting, his forefinger bent backward on the folio which had come from the famous press of Nuremberg. Then he added these mysterious words: "Alas! alas! small things come at the end of great things; a tooth triumphs over a mass. The Nile rat kills the crocodile, the swordfish kills the whale, the book will kill the edifice."

—Victor Hugo, *Notre-Dame de Paris*

CHAPTER EIGHTEEN

To (Pre)Serve and Protect

Tony Amodeo

More is demanded to produce one wise man today, than seven for-merly; and more is needed to deal with a single individual in our times, than with a whole people in the past.

—Baltasar Gracian, 1653

A librarian's traditional duties are to collect, preserve, organize, and make accessible knowledge in all its forms. Those forms have multi-plied, and libraries are doing a lot of organizing—not only of what they hold in-house, but also of what they have online access to. Aggregators (sometimes spelled "aggravators") do some organizing within individual databases, usually giving a list of journals they index and titles they present in full text. At least as of the last revision. At least as of the last time they promised. We don't always find what they promised, as titles come in and go out of databases with little, if any, notification—at least until a patron moans and complains that the promised article can't be found in the database. You check; the patron is right. Sometimes the database just isn't up to date, full-text-wise; sometimes it's a month behind and sometimes a year. And sometimes the title just disappears.

Yet the implication of the aggregator's journal list is that the journal will be available, and some libraries, especially those hard-pressed for space, have dropped paper subscriptions covered by their online services. But as the recent literature questions, can we really trust an aggregator, or the publisher who sells the rights to a journal, to keep the journal available for posterity? (For prosperity is already a given.) Some libraries cope by annually buying microfilm copies of important periodicals as a backup in case an aggregator goes out of business, drops a title, gets dropped by a publisher, and so forth. Academically controlled sites such as JSTOR and Project Muse, as well as possible preservers of cast-off periodicals such as the Center for Research Libraries, ATLA, and digitally speaking, OCLC, give some hope of future preservation, but one never knows for sure. A bad recession hits, and we may become ravenous users of interlibrary loan in hopes of supplying copies of journal articles no longer available via online subscription—if enough copies remain. Other challenges have been raised by recent court decisions regarding freelance writers' copyright rights on articles sold by publishers to aggregators for distribution over the Internet. Some publishers and aggravators (that variant spelling I mentioned) have deleted all articles by freelance writers who might have to be paid a couple of pennies for reuse of their articles. And these are the folks we trust to preserve erstwhile library resources forever?

Those old books and bound serials are looking better and better. Let's hope they'll be around for a while. And yet, what are librarians doing to make sure that they will be? Now that elementary education no longer includes the traditional lesson on how to open a new book without damaging the binding (do librarians still know?); now that almost everyone has begun treating academic books like last year's telephone book (riffle, riffle, rip, riffle); now that the "hook and yank" method of taking books off the shelf has replaced the gentler "slide and lift" method; now that people pick up heavy books by one cover, despite the fact that bindings are weaker than ever; will the books on our shelves survive for even our "term in office"?

Where We Are

Are librarians as responsible for this decline as our in-a-rush throw-away-mentality patrons? Maybe we need to think about that one.

My grandfather built things to last, the old-fashioned way. When he fixed something, it was a repair that lasted and that usually improved on the original. Once, his old three-headed spinning lawn sprinkler wore out. After he fixed it—and made it taller so it would cover a wider area—you could have used it for a car jack.

Publishers' bindings aren't usually like that. While some firms still give you your money's worth—sewn signatures, flexible long-life glues, and a cover hinge that lasts—bindings, even the fancy ones, are generally pretty shoddy. Funny how the heavier and larger the book (like those hundred-dollar-plus art books and science texts on heavy paper), the weaker and flimsier the cover hinges generally are. A good library binder's rebinding, like my grandfather's repairs, are often much stronger than the original. Too bad rebound volumes are not as pretty, and too bad the binder often has to trim down the ungenerous gutter before binding, leading to the "crunch" sound at the photocopier when patrons want to make sure they get all the text.

Librarians notice such things and have even written protest letters to publishers. I once opted not to buy multiple copies of a well-known, somewhat costly, Bible commentary (and later of a dictionary from the same firm) back in the late 1980s because the binding was bound to fail. Like the old nineteenth-century Caoutchouc bindings, the area to be bound was basically dipped in a liquid and then allowed to harden. Of course, the hardened inflexible glue used would crack open and the pages fall out after any use at all, little better than a cheap paperback—in fact, usually a little worse. I wrote letter after letter. Somebody had a good laugh. Needless to say, pages started falling out of the volume after the first time someone photocopied a few pages. But I bought four copies of their competitor's product, which were sewn and are still in use.

Sometimes publishers do listen to librarians. Great progress was made in book preservation when, after years of coaxing and convincing, American publishers followed their European colleagues and began using long-lived nonacidic/nonalkaline paper for their academic books, indicated by that nice infinity sign on the title page overleaf. (As to whether the publishers only did this because they learned that acidic paper pulp was eating up their expensive machines, rather than because of the multiyear campaign by librarians, I choose to remain diplomatically mute.)

Of course, there is no infinity sign on bindings.

Given the status of commercial bookbinding, how careful are we to shelve all books properly, from the moment they leave the packing box, through acquisitions and cataloging procedures, to circulation carts and the library stacks? What kind of book return units do we have? The higher quality kind that lessens abrasion and prevents an actual "drop," or the "usual" kind that lets books fall one upon the other willy-nilly, from a harmful distance?

Where We Should Be

Ideally, we all train our staffs and student workers to ensure that every row of books, whether on a cart or on a shelf, is shelved upright and well-supported by a properly placed bookend. We know, and teach our fellow workers, that a book that leans to one side or the other is under extraordinary structural strain, resulting in warped and weakened bindings. A row of leaning books is more likely to fall to the floor, but even just sitting there the bindings start to pull apart. So we train our student shelvers to constantly monitor and correct the situation as they move around the library.

We can have special horizontal shelving to accommodate very large books, which we lay flat, only three or four on each shelf, to avoid undue pressure, and we remove them one book at a time instead of trying to drag out the one needed from the bottom or middle. Shelving smaller oversize books separately helps us compress shelf space, but also avoids the kind of uneven weight distribution that makes larger books fall over and causes smaller items to be crushed by their neighbors. Larger books that don't quite fit are shelved spine down, so gravity won't tear the text out of the covers; we can place the label so it is upright on the front cover and easily readable by patrons.

We can protect fragile, small, and threatened materials with special covers, binders, or boxes. We can insulate books with experimental or abrasive covers (whether an early binding with metal bosses or the latest metal-armor-clad pop star photofest) with stiff boards or other protection to avoid abrading books they come in contact with.

We can also inspect all incoming microform before discarding our printed volumes, lest a manufacturer's bad master deprive future generations of needed text. We can store our magnetic tape materials (videos and cassette and reel-to-reel) in "played," rather than rewound condition, so that we don't introduce damaging stress. We need to redub these materials on a regular schedule, lest the information be lost by normal deterioration (as was the case with Twyla Tharp's video archive; ten years of documented performances turned to video "snow"). And we can maintain and clean our equipment with undying regularity to keep from harming what they play.

Before discarding a run of periodicals, we can check to make sure some other library in our part of the country holds and will keep it or will accept our volumes; or we check with the Center for Research Libraries, ATLA, or some other preservation program, just to be sure they're not missing one of the very volumes we're about to recycle.

We respect the health of our collections and of our patrons. To be consistent, our staffs and we librarians don't eat or drink in our public areas; nor do we indulge in our offices, knowing that we cannot expect our patrons to respect our rules if we don't. We won't tempt our student workers or staff with candy or cookies except in a designated, separate eating area away from all library materials. We make sure that the maintenance staff gets rid of all food and drink refuse daily from the staff kitchen and from the areas where sneaky patrons may indulge. We do this because we prefer a little self-discipline to the alternative of lacing our buildings and materials with pesticides because we let our guard down. We respect the access rights of patrons with allergies, sensitivities, asthma, and compromised immunity by not making our libraries hostile to their health with pesticides. We are careful to select only new carpeting, carpet glues, and furniture that don't emit toluene or other avoidable toxins, for the same reason: no "sick building" syndrome.

We should do our best to educate our users to avoid behavior harmful to our collections, whether in our instruction sessions or by means of signs, posters, and exhibits. We should teach alternatives for those behaviors, or give patrons alternatives. For example, we can distribute thin paper bookmarks librarywide, instead of just pouting over dog-earing, highlighting, and sticky notes and bemoaning bindings broken from using notebooks or pens as bookmarks.

And we must recognize that we, the librarians, staff, and student workers, consciously or unconsciously, teach our patrons how to respect and treat library materials by our own actions. In every department, we model good behavior and the careful handling of books, media, serials, microform—and each other.

None of this should be new to any professional librarian, especially in an academic library. Every library- or information-science program worth its salt should include, or should have included, all the major functions and responsibilities of the profession in its core curriculum: to acquire, to organize, to make accessible, and to preserve for future generations. Yet, I doubt if any librarian outside a special-collections environment (and even a few there) who reads the preceding paragraphs can say, "Yes, we're doing everything right." If you're implementing even half the above, you're doing relatively well compared to many. On the other hand, if you think, like some pundits, that paper collections are on their way out and that librarians need not be custodians, please think again.

Access, rather than preservation, has been the focal point of libraries for quite some time. But the less we preserve, the more we undercut eventual access. Librarians began to make progress in seeing this connection in the 1970s and 1980s. Even though library-education programs were slow to see the light, library-preservation networks and information-sharing cooperatives began to appear across the spectrum of libraries. Then came the new technology, which diverted all attention and many budgets in this new, demanding direction. Some of the major research libraries cut out good programs that were just beginning to have a positive effect on information survival. Positions changed or were cut altogether.

The situation isn't hopeless. Librarians in the know are providing the means for others to learn those lessons skipped in library school, both via print and online resources. In the last few years, excellent things have been happening. Consider the marvelous compilation *Promoting Preservation Awareness in Libraries* that came out in 1997, for example. Browse the California Preservation Clearinghouse (cpc.stanford.edu), Conservation OnLine (CoOL) (palimpsest.stanford.edu), or the Disaster Preparedness Clearinghouse on the American Library Association's website. There's something for everybody, and big improvements can be made by expending almost nothing but a little effort on our part.

Future Trendiness?

However, for better or worse (you tell me!) libraries and their collections depend on nonlibrary folk for their survival. The price of survival is eternal vigilance—and a lot of persuading. Library administrations have to constantly campaign to keep penny-wise and value-foolish operations staff from turning off the HVAC system on weekends and school holidays, because the few bucks saved come at the high cost of aging the entire collection prematurely, including all those irreplaceable academic titles. With the average price of an academic volume now over fifty dollars, before processing costs, accumulating even a little plenary damage throughout a collection of 100,000 volumes really costs quite a lot.

Can we avoid giving in to the temptation to even think about turning our libraries into coffee shops or cafeterias just to get a few more bodies into the library? Unfortunately, recent articles have been pushing this idea, supporting the belief that students, cluelessly content with what they can get online, have to be bribed and cajoled to step into the library. To quote Pierce Butler, "Your heart is in the right place, but you are forever saying things that give aid and comfort to the enemy."[1] Sadly, those who read such articles superficially, or with their own preconceptions or interests in mind, are likely to say, "Aha! Libraries don't need additional space!" A half-understood point from such articles becomes a slogan for those who want to justify cutting financial support, joining the It's-all-on-the-Internet-so-we-don't-need-libraries cabal. It isn't easy getting these people to listen to the fact that our volumes, unlike the turnover stock at the nearest Borders or Barnes & Noble, are meant to last for as close to forever as we can manage. Once they have their minds made up, it becomes even more difficult. But we must get them to listen.

Don't get me wrong: digitized and online information, especially periodical indexes, short abstracts, and full-text articles, bibliographies, reference works, statistics and the like, are very desirable for both convenience and multiplicity of access, and they are an integral part of today's library services. But despite the best efforts of self-interested outsiders to convince the world otherwise ("We can spend less on the library because everything is going digital—so let's spend it on X and Y instead"), no one without a high level of masochistic self-hatred will ever read the full text of Moby Dick—nor Dickens, Fielding, Dostoevsky, Proust, Homer, Dante, Cervantes, Joyce, Kazantzakis, Achebe, Firdausi, Lao-Tzu, the Mabharata, or even The Little Prince—off a computer screen with enthusiasm and not wish instead for a well-designed, old-fashioned book. (Ask NetLibrary and generations of microfilm users.) The tactile and visual-tactile aspects of reading a well-designed, well-printed text are special and specific. The retrospective mass of existing scholarly books, plus the vast majority of future academic monographs—which will be printed materials—are important parts of the heritage with which we are entrusted. If we give in to pressures from without or from within our own institutions to give up on books or to give them up in favor of fleeting substitutes, the world will be a poorer place. We don't want future generations to say that "digitization was to libraries what Attila was to culture."

We all know that, although there can be a great library without a university, there can be no great university with a mediocre library. And a great library means books—old ones as well as new ones. And lots of them.

How did I find the quote I used at the beginning of this essay? It is in a book, a book published in 1945, before I was born. I inherited it in the 1970s. The original owner, my wife's great-aunt Ruth, had taken care of it. I take care of it. It's still in good shape.

Note

1. "Butler, Pierce," ALA *World Encyclopedia of Library and Information Services*, 2nd ed. (Chicago: ALA, 1986).

Brother Librarian groaned as yet another lead-sealed cask was rolled out of storage for unsealing. Armbruster was

not impressed by the fact that the secular scholar, in two days, had unraveled a bit of a puzzle that had been lying around, a complete enigma, for a dozen centuries.

To the custodian of the Memorabilia, each unsealing represented another decrease in the probable lifetime of the contents of the cask, and he made no attempt to conceal his disapproval of the entire proceeding. To Brother Librarian, whose task in life was the preservation of books, the principal reason for the existence of books was that they might be preserved perpetually. Usage was secondary, and to be avoided if it threatened longevity.

—Walter M. Miller, Jr., *A Canticle for Leibowitz*

CHAPTER NINETEEN

Will Time Tame This Tyrant, Too?

Martin Raish

Any sufficiently advanced technology is indistinguishable from magic.

—Arthur C. Clarke

Imagine a communications product about which it has been said, "No art or science has ever, nor probably ever can, touch the lives of all the people more intimately." Or one that promises to be a "new, inspiring and powerful resource . . . at the disposal of civilization." Or that "answers the call for more liberal education of nations" as well as offering "a richer and more complete home-life." Would you jump at the chance of participating in this wonderful new world?

The good news is that you already have. This technology is radio. And our ease and familiarity with this now common communications medium might provide encouragement in dealing with the oft-felt tyranny of a newer "inspiring and powerful resource," the World Wide Web.

Today, thousands of radio stations send out billions of messages around the clock—music of all conceivable sorts, religious discourses, news, weather information, stock quotes, sports scores, traffic reports, and so forth. Yet we have learned to deal almost unconsciously with this part of the "information explosion." We do not fret over listening to one station instead of another. We probably don't even consider the presets on our car radio as "filters." (They are just "bookmarks.") We are adept at switching stations in an instant so as to find our favorite music or block out annoying talk-show hosts. We know how to ignore most commercials and to pay attention only to those for products or services we need. We have tamed the beast called "radio information glut."

This domestication has taken time, however. Eighty years ago radio was as intimidating to its users as the Web is to many people today. A fascinating and instructive glimpse of how far we have come can be seen in *Radio Enters the Home*[1], a book published by the Radio Corporation of America (RCA) in June 1922, barely a year and a half after the first commercial radio broadcast on November 2, 1920.

What might we learn if we were to read its radiant declarations substituting the phrase "the World Wide Web" for the word "radio"? As the Web has "entered our homes" over the past few years, have we not heard breathtaking descriptions similar to the (anonymous) RCA writer's description of a technology that "travels swift as light" and "on wings of ether" so its "magic touch" can relieve isolation and neglect?

The book was intended for "those who desire to be entertained with radio concerts, lectures, [and] dance music." The new technology was taking the country by storm. Life was being "made over for boys and girls, their fathers and mothers, the strong and well, the blind and the bedridden." Anyone, "without experience or study, [could] enjoy the new national resource":

> With broadcasting rapidly reaching a national and comprehensive stage, the time is not far distant when every home in the United States, from hut to mansion, will be equipped to "listen in" while the Government

makes its reports of crop and weather conditions, while the news of the day is briefly recited, while statesmen plead for united action, while famous artists sing to a larger audience than they have ever known, while splendid bands and orchestras inculcate the taste for music.

Other sections of the book offer equally refreshing food for thought. One presents a list of parts and equipment for the radio enthusiast, much like a modern mail-order computer catalog. It offers a large selection of accessories: batteries and battery chargers, devices to boost reception and power, and speakers to enhance the listening experience. Another extols the benefits of the portable radio (illustrated by "a typical Boy Scout Troop about to depart for a Saturday morning's winter march," complete with one boy carrying a receiver in his knapsack) and stresses its light weight (less than fifteen pounds).

The book also teaches us something about jargon. It offers to sell me a "potentiometer," but even after a brief explanation—it is used to achieve "proper detector action" to give an "increase of signal audibility"—I'm still not sure exactly what it does or why I would want one. Do our explanations ever leave our library patrons feeling the same way?

The author provides a small glossary of radio terms, and some entries are both nostalgic and instructive. "Tuning," which today is a simple matter of spinning a dial or pushing a button, is defined as "the act of altering capacity or inductive values in a radio circuit so as to bring the circuit into resonance with an external source of similar character." How many complex Web operations have become, or are in the process of becoming, similarly invisible?

One page in the book is a list of fifty three-letter abbreviations "to be used in radio communication," as approved by the International Radiotelegraphic Convention. For example, QRV means "are you ready?" and QSR means "will you forward the radiotelegram?" How different are these from our modern chat notations such as TTFN or LOL? Or the "smiley faces" that appear so frequently?

Finally, here are three illustrations from the book that are amusing in their innocence but also eerily prescient of the computer world we now inhabit.

Figure 19.1. "The American Boy has taken to Radio with an enthusiasm probably greater than any other subject of the day." Have times changed?

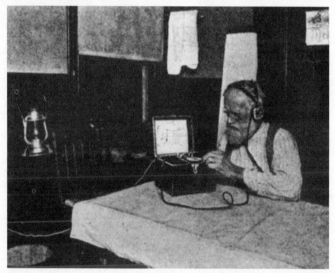

Figure 19.2. "The farmer located within easy distance of a broadcasting station may use Aeriola, Jr. to advantage for the reception of market and weather reports." Could we replace the farmer with a day trader, sports junkie, or travel planner sitting at a workstation looking for similar "advantages?" The farmer needed to be near a broadcast station; all we need is easy access to the Web.

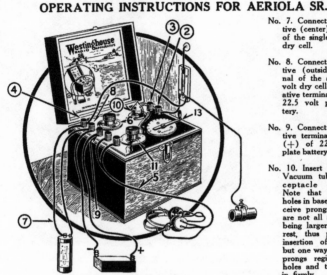

OPERATING INSTRUCTIONS FOR AERIOLA SR.

Text numbers correspond with above diagram.

No. 7. Connect to positive (center) terminal of the single 1.5 volt dry cell.

No. 8. Connect to negative (outside) terminal of the single 1.5 volt dry cell and negative terminal (—) of 22.5 volt plate battery.

No. 9. Connect to positive terminal marked (+) of 22.5 volt plate battery.

No. 10. Insert Aeriotron Vacuum tube in receptacle provided. Note that the four holes in base which receive prongs of tube are not all alike, one being larger than the rest, thus permitting insertion of tube in but one way. Be sure prongs register with holes and then press in firmly.

Numbers Corresponding to Diagram

No. 1. First, refer to accompanying sketch, then erect antenna and place protective device in position as described on page 56.

No. 2. Connect a wire leading from terminal marked R on protective device to binding post indicated by arrow for stations below 350 meters.

No. 3. For stations between 350 and 500 meters, connect the above wire to this post.

No. 4. Connect this post with terminal G of protective device.

No. 5. Connect telephone receivers to these two posts.

No. 6. Turn rheostat as far as it will go toward tail of arrow.

No. 11. Place "Tickler" pointer at zero point of scale.

No. 12. Turn rheostat (6) toward point of arrow until vacuum tube shows dull red. Do not try to burn too brightly as this materially reduces the life of the filament.

No. 13. Rotate tuning handle slowly over the scale, meanwhile listening until sound is heard in the telephone receivers. Adjust to best position, then increase "Tickler" (11) until maximum strength of signal is obtained. If tickler is turned too far toward maximum position, signals will lose their natural tone and reception of telephone signals may become difficult.

Note: This terminal is also connected to terminal G of the protective device.

Figure 19.3. Notice the twelve steps required before you can turn the dial to find the station you want. How reminiscent of installing a new computer or a piece of "user-friendly" software!

Note

1. Original 1922 editions of *Radio Enters the Home*, as well as the 1979 reprint (Vestal Press: New York), are rare, but a photocopy version can be purchased from the Radio Era Archives in Dallas, Texas. It is item number 23334 on its website: http://www.radioera.com.

There are three roads to ruin; women, gambling and technicians. The most pleasant is with women, the quickest is with gambling, but the surest is with technicians.

—Georges Pompidou

Index

The reason why there is no . . . Index added hereunto, is, That every page in the Work is so full of signal Remarks, that were they couched in an index, it would make a volume as big as the Book, and so make the Postern gate to bear no proportion to the Building.
—James Howell, *Discourses Concerning the Precendency of Kings*, 1664

Contributors

Tony Amodeo began his library career at the Newberry Library in Chicago, eventually moving to the department of special collections. He earned his library degree at Rosary College (now Dominican University). After a term as the Illinois cooperative conservation librarian, he worked letterpress with Bruce Beck and Ward Schori in Evanston, Illinois. He then moved to Loyola Marymount University in Los Angeles, where he is associate reference librarian and instruction coordinator at the Charles Von der Ahe Library. He is coauthor of *Introduction to Library Public Services* (1992).

William B. Badke was introduced to librarianship when he took a two-year teaching opportunity in Africa and grew so frustrated with the institutional book collection that he declared himself "librarian." Coming back to Canada for a formal M.L.S., he became a seminary librarian and has held the same position since 1984. He has written two books on research methods, three mystery novels, and a short volume on environmental issues. He always seeks diversity because, he says, "I bore easily." He is currently associate librarian of Trinity Western University for Associated Canadian Theological Schools and Information Literacy.

Amanda Cain earned her B.A. in English literature from The Evergreen State College in Olympia, Washington, and her M.L.S. from the University of Washington. She enjoys getting to know students individually, learning about their interests, and working with them throughout their research process. She is currently humanities/information literacy librarian at West Chester University in Pennsylvania.

Barbara Fister has coordinated the library instruction program at Gustavus Adolphus College since 1987. She is the author of *Third World Women's Literatures: A Dictionary and Guide to Materials in English* (1995), as well as a number of articles on student research processes and the parallels between composition studies and library instruction.

Rebecca S. Graves tried various jobs, including teaching English overseas, before returning to her natal home and acquiring her M.L.S. from the State University of New York at Buffalo in 1994. She is currently the educational services librarian at the J. Otto Lottes Health Sciences Library, University of Missouri, Columbia, where she makes it a habit to speak her mind.

Jon R. Hufford, born in New Haven, Connecticut, has traveled and lived in many places throughout his life. He graduated from high school in Paris, France, and has studied history, foreign languages, and library science at schools as diverse as Miami University, the University of Denver, and Columbia University. He began his library career in a small college in Georgia, has been a cataloger, reference librarian, and microfilm librarian, and is now responsible for a dynamic and growing library instruction program at Texas Tech University.

David Isaacson is humanities librarian and assistant head of reference, Waldo Library, Western Michigan University, Kalamazoo, Michigan.

He has been a librarian there since 1973. He much prefers librarianship to library science.

Margaret Law is associate director of libraries at the University of Alberta and the management liaison to the library's Information Literacy Team. She is interested in how we behave in the workplace and how we meet the changing needs of our users. She has published articles on risk-taking behavior and the need to take personal responsibility in the workplace. She became a librarian because her other career choice, being independently wealthy, didn't seem realistic at the time.

Fred Nesta is director of the libraries at Saint Peter's College in Jersey City and a Ph.D. candidate in the department of information studies at the University of Wales, Aberystwyth.

Monica Ollendorff is the instruction librarian and faculty/staff development/training coordinator in the Irvine Sullivan Ingram Library at the State University of West Georgia. She is a transplanted Georgia Peach, born in Cleveland, previously employed at Michigan State University Library and Saginaw Valley State University Library. In addition to the M.L.S., she also holds an M.S. in social work. She is also a cat lover who is owned by a fifteen-year-old brown tabby named Sheherezade (who at her age has at least 1001 tales to tell) and who looks as if one of her parents was a Maine coon cat. They now live in a loft in what used to be a hosiery mill.

Celia E. Rabinowitz spent some time on the dark side as a faculty member before coming to her senses and becoming a librarian. After studies in the United States and abroad, she settled in 1992 at St. Mary's College of Maryland, a public honors liberal arts college. She is currently director of media, instructional, and public services, so she gets to balance administrative work with instruction, reference, and other duties.

Martin Raish was born and raised in southern California (before the eruption of freeways and strip malls) and eventually earned degrees from schools in four states, including an M.L.S. from Brigham Young University (BYU) and a Ph.D. in art history from the University of

New Mexico. In 1988 he landed at Binghamton University in beautiful upstate New York, where he served as a reference librarian and bibliographer and as coordinator for library instruction. In 1999 he returned to BYU as chair of the department of library instruction and information literacy, and then in June 2002 he moved to BYU–Idaho as director of the David O. McKay Library.

Randy Reichardt is an engineering reference and instruction librarian at the Science and Technology Library and chair of the Information Literacy Team at the University of Alberta. His most recent publication documented an award-winning bibliographic-instruction program offered to undergraduate biology students at the University of Alberta. He is also a professional musician and is addicted to good movies. He became interested in librarianship while teaching guitar to a librarian in the 1970s, and the rest, as they say, is history.

Ilene F. Rockman is the manager of the Information Competence Initiative for the Office of the Chancellor, The California State University (a system of 23 campuses serving 370,000 students with 40,000 faculty and staff). She was previously a library administrator at Cal Poly, San Luis Obispo, and California State University, Hayward, and has been affiliated with the libraries at Washington State University, the Los Angeles Public Library, the Alhambra Public Library, and the University of Southern California. She serves as editor-in-chief of *Reference Services Review*, a quarterly, peer-reviewed journal published by MCB University Press of the United Kingdom, and is active in the American Library Association and its various divisions.

Diana D. Shonrock was born and raised in Iowa and earned her B.S. in education from Iowa State University, her M.S. in "housing" from the University of Iowa during the activist times of the early 1970s, and her M.L.I.S. in 1992. She began teaching "library literacy," including a formal course entitled "Introduction to Library Research Methods," more than twenty years before the terminology was "cool." She is now bibliographer for the College of Family and Consumer Sciences at Iowa State University, involved in too many sections of ALA to name, and editor of *Evaluating Library Instruction* (1996).

Kerry Smith received his M.L.S. from Indiana University, Blooming-ton, in 1997. He earned his M.A. in English from Western Kentucky University, where he taught from 1989 to 1996. He is currently coordi-nator of library instruction services at Mississippi State University Li-braries.

Douglas M. Stehle has been a practicing reference and instruction li-brarian for the past eight years since earning his M.L.I.S. from the Uni-versity of Iowa, where he also earned a B.A. in religion. For five years he served as the library instruction resources coordinator at Leonard H. Axe Library for Pittsburg State University in Kansas. Douglas is cur-rently head of reference and assistant professor in the department of li-brary science for the Duane G. Meyer Library at Southwest Missouri State University in Springfield, Missouri. He lives with his two children and wife, Lisa, who graciously support his professional commitments and remind him that tomorrow is another day. He was part of the Track II group in attendance at ACRL's first Institute for Information Literacy held in Plattsburg, New York, where he met many of the best practi-tioners in the field of library instruction, including Mr. Martin Raish, who kindly invited him to contribute to this book. He would like to ac-knowledge the following people as essential in his development as a li-brarian: Patrick Muckleroy, public services librarian at Western State College of Colorado, the best reference librarian in the mountains and beyond; Robert Walter, dean of learning resources at Pittsburg State University in Kansas, a decisive leader with a vision; and Lynn Cline, head of collections and professor of library science, and Neosha Mackey, associate dean of library services and professor of library science at Southwest Missouri State University, very sagacious and patient men-tors.